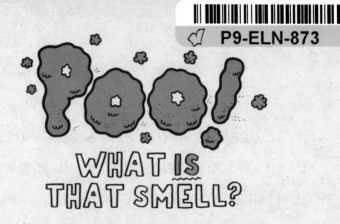

Poo!
WHAT IS THAT SMELL?

Glenn Murphy wrote his first book, *Why Is Snot Green?*, while working at the Science Museum, London. Since then he has written around twenty popular-science titles aimed at kids and teens, including the bestselling *How Loud Can You Burp?* and *Space: The Whole Whizz-Bang Story*.

These days he lives in sunny, leafy North Carolina – with his wife Heather, his son Sean, and two unfeasibly large felines.

Lorna Murphy studied children's book illustration at Cambridge School of Art and created her first picture book, *Maisie's Mountain*, while still there. She lives in Suffolk, sadly without any unfeasibly large cats, but with her partner, who *is* quite tall. When not writing or drawing in her studio, she works in a school library surrounded by inspirational books and people. She also happens to be Glenn's sister.

POO!

WHAT IS THAT SMELL?

EVERYTHING YOU EVER NEEDED TO KNOW ABOUT THE FIVE SENSES

GLENN MURPHY

ILLUSTRATED BY
LORNA MURPHY

MACMILLAN CHILDREN'S BOOKS

First published 2013 by Macmillan Children's Books
an imprint of Pan Macmillan
20 New Wharf Road, London N1 9RR
Associated companies throughout the world
www.panmacmillan.com

ISBN 978-0-330-53852-7

5 7 9 8 6

A CIP catalogue record for this book is available from
the British Library.

Typeset by Nigel Hazle
Printed and bound by CPI Group (UK) Ltd, Croydon CR0 4YY

Thanks to all my family and friends who have continued to support me over the years – in particular Glenn, for making science fun and this collaboration so special. And, of course, to Kevin – lots of love xxx (LM)

INTRODUCTION

This is a book all about **senses**. But hang on a minute – what *are* senses?

Everybody knows there are five senses: **sight**, **smell**, **hearing**, **taste** and **touch**. Easy, right?

Senses give humans (and other animals) information about the world outside their bodies. They are **feelings** or **sensations** that allow us to explore our surroundings, find food, find mates, avoid dangerous predators and pitfalls, and much, much more.

But did you know that *every* animal (and *every* person) in the world sees, hears, smells, tastes and feels things in a slightly different way? We've all heard that dogs have better hearing than humans, and that owls have better eyesight. But did you know . . .

- That bees and pigeons see the world in different colours?
- That the same patch of grass will smell very different to a dog and a cat?
- That if we could hear it, a bat's scream would be louder than a gunshot?
- That spiders can hear through their feet?
- That butterflies can taste things through their feet?
- That some animals (including humans) have more than 20 different senses?

Some animals have bigger eyes, ears and noses than others. Some have no eyes, ears or noses at all. So naturally some will have keener senses than others.

But the really amazing thing is that nothing we see, hear, smell, taste or touch is actually real!

Instead, our senses build up a kind of 'virtual reality' picture of the world around us. So the same world may look completely different when seen by two different animals, or even two different people. How the world looks, sounds, smells, tastes and feels depends on how our brains and senses work.

In other words, the world is only as real as our senses make it.

If that sounds crazy, then hold on tight, as in this book we'll be exploring all this and more. We'll experience the world through the **eyes of a falcon**, through the **ears of a bat**, through the **nose of a bloodhound**, through the **taste buds of a butterfly** and through the soft, deadly **touch of a spider**.

Sounds like fun, right?

Trust me – it'll look, smell and feel like fun too!

Right, then.

On with the show . . .

CHAPTER 1:
SIGHT

COMMON SENSE

How Do We See?

To humans, eyesight (or vision) is probably the most important sense of all. We get most of our information about the world around us from our eyes. When we're blindfolded, or we find ourselves in pitch darkness with no light to see by, we feel lost and scared. We depend on our eyes so much that it's hard to imagine life without them.

But what's actually inside those two, strange, gooey little balls in your head?

How do eyes *work*, and how do we *see* things?

Are they like little video cameras, sending pictures to the brain?

Well, in a way, yes – they are.

Like **video cameras**, eyes convert rays of light into **electrical signals**. Our brains piece those signals together in order to build pictures and images in our heads. But unlike video cameras, which record things, eyes are there to help humans (and other animals) look for things. Stuff like food, dangerous predators and the way home. A good pair of eyes, connected to a handy brain, lets animals hunt, seek, sneak, grab, pounce, aim and move about without getting hurt.

How Did Eyes Evolve?

Eye-spots

The simplest types of eyes in the animal kingdom are found in microscopic animals like **Euglena**. These animals have tiny 'eye-spots' that contain special, light-sensing proteins. When light hits these spots, the proteins inside change shape, which tells the animal that there are rays of light all around it.

With this simple kind of eye, you can tell the difference between **light or dark**, **sunshine or shade**. That's pretty much it. But as it happens, being able to tell the difference between light and dark is a pretty handy trick. For starters, it lets you hide in the dark when bigger, nastier animals are nearby. It also tells you when you're swimming into the light, where you're most likely to find food. And most importantly, it warns you to scarper when you're suddenly covered by the shadow of a hungry, looming bug-hunter!

These simple eye-spots were the first type of eye to appear in the animal world. Animals first evolved them about **530 million years ago**, in the Earth's prehistoric oceans. But as we can all plainly see,* eyes didn't stop developing there.

In the millions of years since, eyes have evolved over 100 times. They've developed in lots of different types of animal – everything from insects and spiders to ostriches and octopuses. The more useful their eyes became, the more animals came to depend on them.

* Get it? See? Heheheh. OK – maybe it wasn't that funny . . .

Eye-patches and Eye-pits

A few million years after eye-spots, **flatworms** and other animals began evolving **eye-patches**. No – not those funny eye-patches you see on **pirates**.* More like patches, or sheets, of **light-sensing cells**. Basically, lots of tiny eye-spots all working together.

With an eye-patch like this, a tiny-eyed flatworm could not only sense shadows of other animals, but also their outlines, or their rough size and shape. This would let one worm tell the difference between a *smaller* worm nearby (which *he* might want to eat) and a *larger* worm (which might want to eat *him*). Again, since this was a very a handy trick, worms with eye-patches tended to do well, and went on evolving into other things.

In some animals (probably mutant worms too), these eye-sheets folded inwards to form little **dents** or **cups**. With this, an animal could not only make out the size and shape of a nearby object, but also which way it was **moving**. Which is obviously very handy, for both hunting and escaping things.

* Although that would look pretty funny. Just imagine the funny movie poster for *Flatworms of the Caribbean* . . .

Evolution of the Eye

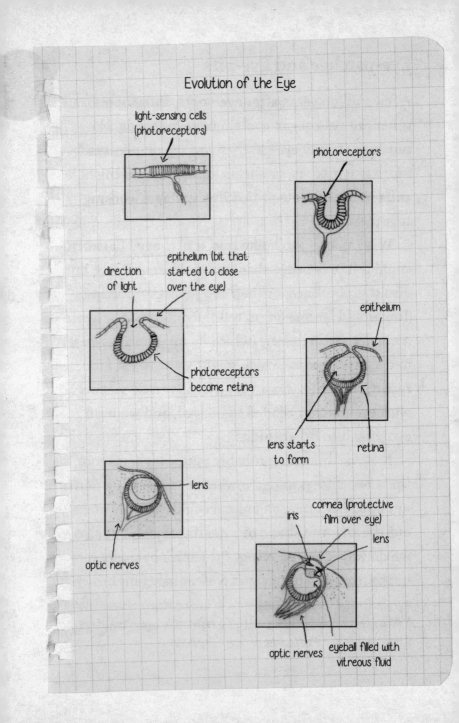

light-sensing cells (photoreceptors)

photoreceptors

epithelium (bit that started to close over the eye)

direction of light

epithelium

photoreceptors become retina

lens starts to form

retina

lens

cornea (protective film over eye)

iris

lens

optic nerves

optic nerves

eyeball filled with vitreous fluid

Eyeballs Everywhere

From there, eye-cups evolved into **eyeballs**. In a few lucky animals, the upper edges of the eye-cups began to close over, leaving just a small hole at the top. Rays of light could then enter through the hole, and fan out to hit a curved sheet of light-sensing cells (called the **retina**) at the back of the eye. You still find this type of '**pinhole eye**' today in ancient animals like the **nautilus** – a big, shrimp-like animal with a rounded shell that lives in the deep sea.

Over time, some of these eyeballs closed over completely. In these closed-off eyeballs, light enters through a clear window instead of a hole. This is called the **lens**, and it also helps to direct (or focus) light on to the light-sensing retina within, just like a glass lens focuses light into a telescope or camera. In some animals, this lens is surrounded by a ring of tiny muscles, called an **iris**. In **humans**, this is the coloured bit that surrounds the dark hole (or **pupil**) in the centre of the eye.

The iris gives us our pretty blue, green or brown eye colours. But it does much more than that. The iris focuses the light entering the eye by **stretching**

or squashing the lens – pulling it into more (or less) curved shapes. This allows the eye to focus on objects both near and far, taking snapshots of the whole world around it.

Seeing the *whole world at once* proved to be so handy that *lots of animals* developed eyes like this. These include snakes, fish, lizards, frogs, cats, dogs, birds, monkeys, gorillas and – ta-daa!! – humans. Eyeballs with lenses, irises and retinas are what give us and most other **vertebrates** (or animals with backbones) our keen sense of sight.

Of course, many **invertebrates** (animals without backbones) evolved eyes too. But theirs turned out a bit different. As we'll soon see, **insects**, **spiders** and **crustaceans** have multiple (or **compound**) eyes, while **squid** and **octopuses** have **camera-like** eyes, a bit more like ours.

Yep – eyes have turned out to be a pretty handy thing to have. Which is why they've turned up all over the animal kingdom . . .

Do animals see colours?

You might have heard that only humans can see colours, and that other animals – like cats, dogs, cows and monkeys – are colour-blind. But in fact, that's simply *not true*. Some animals do only see the world in black and white. But others enjoy the same, glorious, multicoloured vision we do, and *some* can even see colours we can't see!

So how does colour vision work?

Well, as we've already learned, the light-sensing patch of cells at the back of an animal's eye is called the **retina**. Within the retina, there are two basic types of light-sensing cells – **rod cells** and **cone cells**. The rods just sense light and dark, while the cones let animals recognize light of different colours.

Now here's the thing: different types of cone cells are triggered by different colours of light. One type of cone reacts to **red** light, another type to **green** and **yellow**, and still another to **blue** light. But not all animals have every type of cone cell in their eye. Which means there are some colours of light that some animals can't see.

So which colours can they see?

Humans (along with most **monkeys**, **apes** and **other primates**) have **three** types of cone cell wedged in their retinas – red, green and blue. So we have **three-colour vision**. That doesn't, of course, mean that we can only see three colours. It means we can see red, green, blue and *every colour of the rainbow* in between. Thanks to our mix of coloured cone cells, we get to enjoy yellow, orange, brown and purple too.

Sadly, not all mammals are quite as lucky as us, eye-wise. Most have only **two-colour** vision. These animals include **cats**, **dogs** and farm animals like **cows**, **goats** and **sheep**. All these animals' eyes lack red cone cells, so they can only see in shades of blue, green and yellow. Your pet dog, then, doesn't see the world in black and white, like he's looking at some old photograph. But he doesn't quite see the world the way that you do, either.

Many **nocturnal** mammals – those that hunt and scamper around by night – have lost their blue cone cells too. So they have **single-colour** vision. The same goes for sea mammals like **whales**, **dolphins** and **manatees**. Again, they don't see in black and white – it's more like shades of light and dark green, a bit like what you'd see through those **night-vision** goggles that soldiers wear.

14

Amazingly, many **reptiles**, **amphibians**, **birds** and **sharks** have **four** (or *even five*) types of cone cell in their eyes so they are able to see colours (or rather, types of light) that we cannot see. Many **birds**, for example, can see **ultraviolet (UV) light**. This lets them see patterns of light on flowers, trees and grassy hillsides that are invisible to humans. **Snakes**, meanwhile, have extra cone cells that can detect invisible, **infrared (IR) light** given off by warm objects. With this special, snakey, **super-vision**, a pit viper can pick out the warm body of a quivering mouse in complete darkness. Good news for the snake; bad news for mousey . . .

So why do animals see colours at all?

Seeing colours comes in very handy for a whole host of different reasons. **Primates** (monkeys, apes and humans) probably evolved their three-colour vision for **spotting fruit** hidden in leafy trees. **Birds** use their four-colour vision to **navigate** during long migrations, and to **choose the healthiest mates** (who may have the most brightly coloured feathers). Many **reptiles** (including the dinosaurs) probably used their three-, four- or five-coloured vision for the same purpose.

Nocturnal mammals like mice and rabbits have little use for colour vision in darkness. Nor do whales and dolphins, as colours are dulled where they live beneath the waves. So simple, single-colour vision does the job well enough. For other mammals – two-colour (blue-green) vision is good enough for finding food, staying with the herd or pack, and spotting predators hidden in long grasses.

So we humans should count ourselves lucky – we get to see the world in colours most other animals don't get to see. Then again, we don't get to see heat trails or the beautiful, invisible patterns on flower petals, either . . .

Life in 3D

Not only do humans enjoy the world in glorious technicolour, we also get to see it in amazing, life-like 3D! Again, this makes us the lucky ones, as not all animals do . . .

To see the world in three dimensions, you have to be able to see the same scene from two slightly different angles. The simplest way to do this is with two eyes, pointed in the same direction, but spaced apart from each other on your face. This, in fact, is how we humans see in 3D.

Try it for yourself.

Look out of the window, pick a nearby object, and close each eye in turn so that you're looking at it first with just the left eye, then the right.
Now pick an object much further away – like a building across the street, or a tree at the end of your garden – and repeat the experiment.

When you gaze at the 'near' object, it seems to move or shift a bit as you flick from left to right eye. But the 'far' object pretty much stays put, right?

This is because each eye is looking at these objects from a slightly different viewpoint. The nearer the object, the bigger the angle between the two viewpoints. Your brain then uses this angle to judge the distance from your eyes to the thing you're looking at. This type of double-eyed, 3D vision is called stereoscopic vision.

Handily enough, **humans**, **chimps**, **gorillas**, **monkeys**, **lemurs** and other **primates** do have **two forward-facing eyes**. *Most* other animals, though, do not. **Horses**, **cows** and **sheep** – like most mammals – have **eyes on the sides of their heads**. So to judge the distance to an object, they have to flick their heads from side to side to look at the same scene from two different angles.

If you've ever been for a walk in the countryside, near a farmer's field, you may have noticed that once they've spotted you, horses, cows or sheep swing their heads from side to side as you approach. Well, this explains why. They're trying to judge how far away you are (and whether or not they need to leg it if you get too close).

So why don't *all* animals have 3D vision?

Because many don't need it. Horses, cows, antelopes and other grazing, herding **herbivores** evolved eyes on the sides of their heads to (literally) **keep an eye out for predators** like wolves, lions and hyenas. Each eye has a wide angle of vision, which makes it very hard for a lion or wolf to sneak up on herbivores – especially if they stay in herds and watch each other's backs while they graze.

Sneaky meat-eating hunters (or **carnivores**) evolved forward-facing eyes and 3D vision to help them to the **judge the distance to their prey** before they pounce, and to keep their **eyes on their target** while they're giving chase. Have a think about that the next time your pet cat locks two hungry eyes on your ankles . . .

Advanced 3D

Humans, chimps, monkeys and other primates all evolved from animals that lived in trees – jumping and swinging between branches to avoid meeting dangerous predators down on the ground. So we evolved our forward-facing eyes and 3D vision not for hunting, but for **tree-swinging acrobatics**. A monkey or lemur that couldn't judge the distance to the next branch was in for a nasty fall. So the ones with good 3D vision survived better, and passed on their advanced eyesight to us.

As for birds, reptiles, and other animals, some have 2D vision, others 3D, while others are somewhere in between. Most **birds** have eyes that face both forwards and to the side, with patches of overlapping 3D vision to the front (for hunting) and patches of wide-angle 2D vision to the side (for spotting sneaky hunters). The big exceptions to this rule are **owls**, which have two forward-facing eyes and incredibly powerful 3D vision. This makes them **deadly night-time hunters**, and the terror of every mouse, vole and scampering rodent in the land. Once they lock their wide-eyed gaze upon you, there's nowhere to run and nowhere to hide.

Eeeeeeek!

ANIMAL SENSE

Fight, run or hide?

We've already learned that many predators –
including lions, tigers and birds of prey – hunt
their prey with keen, all-seeing eyes. It's often said
that **prey animals** in danger have two choices:
either they fight for their lives, or they run away.
Biologists call this '**fight or flight**'. But if the
hunter depends mostly on vision to find you, then
you have a third choice. Hide.

In the animal world, **camouflage** is a way of
fooling hunters and predators. It allows prey
animals to hide from hungry eyes by blending in
with the colours and shapes of their environment.
Hiding is a very successful tactic for prey animals –
it usually works a lot better than trying to fight off
a lion, tiger or golden eagle. So not surprisingly,
camouflage is very common, and found in almost
every part of the animal kingdom.

Which animals are the masters of disguise?

Insects are certainly in the running for that title. Many **moths** and **butterflies** have wing markings and colours that that are almost identical to those of the tree trunks and leaves they perch on. **Stick insects** and **leaf insects** can look so much like twigs and leaves that they're almost impossible to spot when they sit motionless upon them.

Many frogs and toads use incredible disguises too. **Green tree frogs** are the same colour as the bright rainforest leaves they cling to, while **leaf frogs** have orangey-brown skin the colour of fallen leaves, complete with curling points, edges and veins.

Reptiles, too, are fond of hiding and lurking. **Lizards** mimic sticks, **tree snakes** coil around branches like vines, and **chameleons** famously change their skin colour from brown to green as they creep among trees and bushes.

Some mammals and birds change colour from season to season – growing new coverings of fur or feathers to better hide against the changing landscape. **Arctic hares**, **fur seals** and **ptarmigans** go from brown to white as the snows cover their lands, as do the **Arctic foxes** that hunt them.

Sea-dwelling animals use camouflage too. **Jellyfish** and **plankton** have transparent bodies to make them harder to spot underwater, as do many baby fish right after hatching. Many **adult fish** have skins and scales that are darker on the upper side and paler on the underbelly. This is called *countershading*. It keeps the fish hidden from birds peering down into the dark depths from above, and also hides them from bigger fish peering up at the brightly lit surface from below.

Of course, just as in the human world, the hunters use camouflage too. **Polar bears**, hidden by their thick, white coats, hunt seals on the Arctic ice. **Sharks** and **killer whales** use dark-and-light countershading to hide their bodies from their fishy prey (along with human fishing and whaling boats) in the water. And **praying mantises** sit patiently among leaves, twigs and flower petals – their bodies blending perfectly with their surroundings as they await for their prey to creep by.

Hiding in plain sight

Camouflage is a tactic used mostly by animals that live in places with lots of nooks, crannies and hidey-holes, like forests, woodlands and swamps. After all, hiding only works if you have *somewhere to hide*. To be well camouflaged, an animal needs a background of **trees**, **plants**, **leaves**, **rocks** or other objects to be camouflaged *against*. Without them, it's a bit like playing hide-and-seek in a big room with no furniture – even if you *are* the same colour as the walls and carpet, chances are, you'll get spotted pretty quickly. So what about all the animals that live on open plains, hillsides and grasslands where there's nowhere to hide? What do they do? Well, they tend to use a different tactic – **herding.**

Don't herds make bigger, meatier targets for predators?

Living in herds helps sheep, cows, horses, zebras, antelopes and a whole host of other animals stay *safer* from predators.

Herding makes it difficult for a predator to pick out one single animal from all the rest. When a lioness charges at a pack of wildebeest or antelope, the herd stampedes and there's dust and hoofs flying everywhere. While there should be lots of nice, juicy wildebeest to choose from, in the confusion, the lioness finds it **hard to pick a target**, and has to wait for one 'straggler' to stray from the herd before she can zero in on it and bring it down.

Some animals, like **zebras**, combine the tactics of herding *and* camouflage to make picking a tasty target even more confusing. Ever wonder why zebras have black-and-white stripes, when they live among the mostly brown-and-green colours of the African plains? It's not so they can hide against the background (which clearly wouldn't work). It's so that they can hide among each other. A herd of stripey zebras presents a confusing optical illusion to lions and hyenas. The stripes disguise the outline of each animal in the herd, making it hard to tell where one zebra ends and another one begins, or which way they might be facing. This makes it especially difficult for their predators to select a target, let alone predict which way they might run once the chase begins.

Safety in numbers

In the air, **small birds** use similar tactics – **flocking** together to confuse the hawks and falcons that hunt them. And underwater, **fish** confuse attacking sharks and dolphins by swimming together in **shoals**.

But that's not the only reason prey animals like to stay together. Herding, flocking and shoaling also *combines* the senses of all the animals in the group. It gives them many, many *extra pairs of eyes* (not to mention *ears* and *noses*) with which to detect an approaching danger. When a herd of zebras or antelope stop to graze, some keep their heads up to watch for creeping lions while the others munch away at the grass, head down. When a flock of sparrows is attacked by a sparrowhawk, the birds nearest to the swooping predator can chirp a warning to the birds behind, allowing the flock to dodge, open up or separate to let the attacker whizz past.

As the old saying goes, there's **safety in numbers**, and it all works better than you'd think.

Do flies have eyeballs?

No, they don't. Instead, they have hundreds of tiny eye-tubes, all bundled together to make compound (or multi-part) eyes. At first glance, insect eyes look like little footballs. We use the phrase 'bug-eyed' for a reason – it's as if they have two, huge eyeballs bulging out of their heads.

If you use a microscope to look closely, you'll see that each 'eyeball' is made up of hundreds of tiny hexagons. These hexagons are called **facets**, and each one is a tiny lens that sits at the end of a long, light-gathering **eye-tube**. Each eye-tube is like a miniature telescope. The tiny, glass-like lens at one end funnels light into a tube behind, which is lined with special, light-sensing proteins. So each insect eye is like a bundle of telescopes, all roped together and pointing into the insect's brain.

Of course, the brain doesn't 'look' through these little telescopes at all. Instead, the eye-tubes send signals to the insect's brain through tiny nerves, building up a picture of the world outside.

So what does the world look like to an insect?

To an insect, the world looks like a big mosaic – like those pictures you see on ancient Roman floors, made up of hundreds of tiny, coloured tiles. Because each eye-tube points in a slightly different direction, it's as if the insect is looking at the world through hundreds of tiny, glass windows.

Human eyes have just one lens each, and we can change the shape of it by pulling it about with tiny muscles inside the eyeball. This lets us focus on objects both near and far. But the lenses in a compound eye can't be moved. This means most insects are **short-sighted**. They can see close objects fairly well, but distant objects appear blurry and out of focus. Unlike humans, insects can't wear specs or contact lenses to correct their vision (that would be kind of funny, but alas, no one has invented bug specs yet). So they stay short-sighted for life.

But if a fly's vision is so blurry, why are they so good at dodging fly-swatters?

Compound eyes might be rubbish for reading number-plates and viewing Van Gogh paintings, but they're very good at picking out movement. As an object – like an attacking bird, hand or fly-swatter – whizzes between the 'windows' of the fly's vision, it triggers a chain of nerve signals in each eye-tube. This tells the fly it'd better wing it, sharpish. And because the eye-tubes point in different directions (including straight up and straight back along the fly's body), a fly can see things above and behind itself, making it seem as if it has eyes in the back of its head!

29

BIG SENSE

Which animals have the biggest eyes?

The animal with the largest eyes in the world is the giant or colossal squid. **Giant squid** reach up to 17m (56 feet) in length, and the largest found to date had an eye that measured 25cm (10 inches) across, or about the size of a large dinner plate. For many years, biologists thought that the even larger **colossal squid** did not exist. But in 2007, a fishing trawler in New Zealand accidentally netted a colossal squid that measured over 10m (36 feet) in length, with an eye diameter of **28cm (11 inches)**. Which didn't seem so amazing until scientists realized *it was just a baby one*. It's now thought that *adult* colossal squid could

25cm

grow up to three times larger, with eyes over a *foot* (30cm) across.

Other big-eyed animals include the blue whale, ostriches and ichthyosaurs.

Blue whales have eyeballs the size of soccer balls – even the bit you can see from the outside measures **15-20cm (6-8 inches)** across.

Ostriches have the largest eyes of any living bird, at **5cm (2 inches)** across – around twice the size of a human eye.

Ichthyosaurs (or 'fish-lizards') were giant, ocean-dwelling reptiles that became extinct around the same time as the dinosaurs. They looked like huge, scaly, toothy dolphins, grew up to 4m (13 feet) in length, and had eyes that measured over **20cm (8 inches)** across.

Best Eyesight on land

Which land animal has the best eyesight?

If you ignore birds, then the prize for best-eyesight-on-land probably goes to the **giraffes**. Their height allows them to see over low-lying trees and bushes, and their keen eyes allow them to see for miles across the open plains and grasslands of Africa.

Many reptiles, though, have pretty good eyesight too. **Chameleons**, in particular, have full-colour vision, and can rotate their eyes in opposite directions. This allows them to hunt for insects with one eye while keeping an eye out for snakes, eagles, cats and other predators. Since each eye can rotate through almost **180 degrees**, the chameleon can see **360 degrees** around its body (which is better even than an owl, which can only turn its head through about 270 degrees).

Which sea animal has the best eyesight?

With the exception of **sharks** and other large hunters, most fish have pretty poor eyesight, and depend more upon touch, hearing and smell to survive. Most whales, dolphins and porpoises don't have great eyesight, either – relying more upon sound to find each other and their prey.

Some of the best eyes beneath the waves actually belong to **octopuses**, **squid** and **cuttlefish**. Many species have good, full-colour vision, and use visual signs and signals to communicate with each other. These species use their fins, bodies and skin to create an incredible range of messages and signals – spreading their bodies flat, or squeezing them into tubes to say 'I'm the boss' or 'OK – you're the boss'. They also curl their tentacles into V-shaped horns to threaten each other, or beckon each other with inviting 'come here' waves.

Squid and **cuttlefish** also ripple their fins in different patterns to send happy or angry messages. And incredibly, some can even use their skin like TV or computer screens.

Just beneath the surface of their skin, squid and cuttlefish have thousands of tiny, coloured spots called 'chromatophores'. Each one is attached to a tiny muscle controlled by the animal's brain, and can be made bigger or smaller in an instant. By shrinking some spots and expanding others, the animal can create blotches, patches and patterns all over its skin, turning its body into one big, multicoloured message-board.

Cuttlefish are especially good at this. They can change their whole skin colour from white or pale yellow to dark brown. They can flash big patches

33

of pink or purple, cover their skins with yellow-and-black tiger stripes, and even paint a big pair of dark, menacing eyes on their backs! Using these and other patterns, cuttlefish chat with their mates, sweet-talk their girlfriends or boyfriends, and threaten and bully their rivals. Most amazingly of all, a single cuttlefish can use different parts of the body to display three or four different messages – all at the same time. This means they can be chatting up a lady-friend with one side of their body, while also using the other side to threaten or warn off two rival males.

Which animal has the most eyes?

Most people believe **spiders** to have the most eyes. While they do have quite a few (spiders and scorpions have 3–6 pairs of eyes, or 6–12 eyes in total), the prize for most eyes actually goes to jellyfish. Deadly, stinging **box jellies** have **24 eyes**, and other jellyfish species may have even more. Also in the underwater category, **giant clams** don't have eyes as such, but they do have hundreds of tiny, photo-sensitive spots lining the fleshy rim of their shells.

As we've already seen, **flies, bees and other insects** have **compound eyes** made up of hundreds (or even thousands) of mini eye-tubes called **ommatidia**. So depending on how you look at it (if you'll pardon the pun), you could say they have two eyes, or over two thousand eyes!

In fact, most insects have compound eyes, as do shrimp, lobsters, and other sea-dwelling **crustaceans**. Different species, though, have different numbers of eye-tubes, giving them a better or worse sense of sight. **Fruit flies** have about 800 tubes per eye, and have fairly good eyesight, while some flea species have just one or two eye-tubes per eye, making them almost blind. **Dragonflies** are probably the sharpest-eyed of all. With up to **30,000** tubes per eye, their keen eyesight makes them ferocious hunters of other flying insects. They're like the eagles of the insect world!

Which animal has the smallest eyes?

Among ocean-dwelling animals, **dinoflagellates** (which are a type of plankton) have primitive eyes so tiny that it's hard to see them even with a microscope. The whole animal measures just **50–70 micrometres** (that's five-hundredths of a millimetre, or a thousandth of an inch) across, so you can imagine how small the eyes must be! Also beneath the waves, copepods – tiny marine animals related to barnacles – have pretty tiny eyes too, which measure less than **half a millimetre** across.

On land, insects tend to have the tiniest eyes. But **bumblebee bats** and **bee hummingbirds** win the small-eye prize for mammals and birds. They're both very fittingly named. At just 25mm (1 inch) in length, bumblebee bats appear more like bees than bats, and their tiny eyes are little more than a millimetre wide. Bee hummingbirds aren't much bigger. At just 5cm (2 inches) in length, they're the world's tiniest birds, and have eyes measuring just a couple of millimetres across. They also build inch-wide nests that look like miniature eggcups.

Which animal has the worst eyesight?

While most animals have been successful because they evolved vision, some have lost their power of sight altogether. As we've already learned, there are **blind cave fish**, **blind salamanders** and even **blind mole rats** that live in total darkness their whole lives. Among those that *can* see, the **Ganges river dolphin** (also known as the **blind river dolphin)** probably has the worst eyesight of any mammal. With eyes like tiny pinpricks and no lens to focus the little light that gets in, even a hefty pair of dolphin spectacles wouldn't do them much good. But since they live in the silty, murky waters of the Ganges, they'd have little use for them anyway. Among reptiles, there is an entire family of **blind lizards (Dibamidae)** which have *eyes covered with skin*. I guess they don't need them much, either!

SPECIAL SENSE

Spy like a bird

Do birds with big eyes have better eyesight?

As you probably know, most birds have good eyesight. At least compared with other animals like insects and mammals. Then again, **ostriches** – the biggest-eyed birds on the planet – don't see as well as **sparrowhawks**, which are far, far smaller. That's because it not just the *size* of the eye that matters, it's what's *inside* it.

In many ways, bird eyes are much the same as ours. They have eyeballs, lenses, irises, pupils, retinas – all the usual stuff. But in other ways, they're quite different.

Not all birds have the huge, scary eyes of an owl or eagle. But in general, their eyes are bigger and heavier in relation to their heads than those of, say, mammals like us. A **human head** is about **100 times bigger and heavier** than a human eyeball.

Meaning that – if you really wanted to – you could cram about 100 eyeballs into one human head.*

A **bird's head**, on the other hand, is only about **5 or 6 times bigger and heavier** than its eyes. This is partly because birds have very thin, lightweight skull bones. But it's also because their eyes take up a large area of their heads and faces.

Extra Eyelids

A person with bird-like eyes would look very strange indeed. Not just because his eyes would look huge, and bulge out of his head, but for other reasons too. Many birds, you see, can't move their eyes at all. While human eyeballs roll around in their sockets to track moving objects, a bird with immovable eyes has to move its whole head to keep a moving object in view.

What's more, most birds have not one, not two, but *three eyelids*. In addition to the standard 'top and bottom' eyelids – which open and close like a clamshell – birds have a third, semi-transparent eyelid called a **blinking** (or **nictitating**) **membrane**. This third eyelid sits behind the other

* It might make a bit of a mess, but hey – it's still possible.

two, and helps to keep the surface of the eye moist and clean. Instead of it flicking up and down, the third, birdy eyelid flicks across the eye from left to right (or vice versa) as it blinks.

Eagle-eyed

Eagles and other sharp-eyed birds of prey get their amazing vision not from the size of their eyeballs (although they are quite large), but from the *number of light-sensing cells* inside.

As we've already learned, the light-sensing cells inside animal eyeballs are called **rod cells** and **cone cells**, and they lie together in a light-sensing patch at the back of the eye called the **retina**. Animals with good eyesight tend to have rather a lot of these cells packed into the retina. In **human** eyes, there are about **200,000** rod and cone cells in every square millimetre of the retina.

Now compare this with an average perching garden bird. The eyes of **sparrows**, **thrushes** and **blue tits** have about **400,000** rod and cone cells per square millimetre of retina. This makes their eyesight roughly twice as powerful as ours. They can see objects from almost twice as far away, or pick out objects – like buzzing insects and tiny seeds in long grass – that are too small for humans to notice.

But that's nothing compared with **birds of prey** such as **falcons**, **eagles** and **buzzards**. The retinas of **buzzards** and **vultures** have up to 1,000,000 rod and cone cells per square millimetre. Most of these cells are clustered together in a tiny patch within the retina called the **fovea**. Humans have a fovea too. For us, it's the bit in the centre of our vision that we use for reading and picking out fine details (the rest of our view remains blurry, and our brains just fill in the missing details by themselves). But in birds, it's like having a powerful magnifying glass or telescope in the centre* of their vision. All together, this makes their vision **5–8** times more powerful than our own, and enables them to spot a hopping rabbit at a distance of over **2 miles (3km)**, or a mouse hiding in long grass from **500 feet (800m)** or more above.

Seeing Secret Colours

Amazingly, birds also have better colour vision than humans do. We might think we can see every colour

---

* Actually, it's a little bit off-centre, but you get the idea.

41

there is. But in fact, most birds can pick out many, many more – including at least two shades that are completely invisible to humans!

They use their colourful, feathered bodies to create an entire language of birdy-y signs and signals. Male **peacocks** fan out their magnificent, colourful tails to chat up female **peahens**. In the Galapagos Islands, **blue-footed boobies** turn their beaks and wingtips towards the sky to chat up their girlfriends. (If they like them, the females respond with funny, slow-motion walks and show the males the bottoms of their big, blue feet).*

Their excellent colour vision is down to cone cells – the colour-sensing cells we met earlier on. So while humans, who only have three types of cone cell, can see red, green, blue and all the colours of the rainbow in between, birds have four or five types of cone cell and can tell the difference between two shades of red (or green, or blue) that would look identical to you and me. Just as some colour-blind

* Male birds of paradise clear a stage (called a lek) in the middle of the forest floor, then strut, dance and do acrobatic flips to impress the watching 'ladies'. Other birds 'talk' about getting together by pairing up and dancing with each other – circling, strutting and bobbing their heads in time.

humans have trouble telling reds and greens apart (but can make out blues and yellows), to birds, all humans are colour-blind to some degree.

What's more, many birds can also see **infrared (IR)** and **ultraviolet (UV)** frequencies of light that are totally invisible to us. This is not just like looking through an infrared camera, where all invisible IR light is converted into a shade of red so that we can see it. Instead, to a bird, these extra colours would be layered *on top of* all the colours we (and it) can already see, revealing beautiful patterns in the landscape that are invisible to human beings. Some birds – like **pigeons**, **terns** and **albatrosses** – probably use these patterns of invisible UV light to navigate, picking out plants and trees with UV patterns over land, or corals and undersea features that reflect UV light out at sea. Others, like **hummingbirds**, use their 'secret vision' to spot UV patterns on the petals and leaves of flowering plants, which the plants use to advertise their tasty nectar and berries.

If we could see the world as a bird does, we would be astonished. It would be like looking down from a soaring aeroplane. The landscape would be

exploding with colours we had never seen. It would be **sharp** enough to zoom in on tiny plants and animals. And it would be woven through with the **secret patterns** and messages of nature.

COMMON SENSE

CHAPTER 2: HEARING

COMMON SENSE

What is hearing, and why do we have it?

Hearing is the newest of our five basic senses. It appeared in animals millions of years after smell, taste, sight and touch. In fact, *hearing is really just a sense of touch that works at a distance*. Ears are basically big, hairy, touch-sensors that allow us to sense ripples in the air or water around us.
So why would we need to do that? What use is sensing air and water ripples?

Well, pretty much anything that moves creates ripples or waves. Underwater, the flip of a fishy fin or the snapping of a shark's jaws creates **ripples in the water**, which can be felt through the skin of nearby animals. On land, padding feet, beating drums and wheezing lungs create ripples too – only *they* do it **in the air around us**. We

call these ripples sound waves. Being able
to feel (or hear) these waves allows
animals to do many of the same
things that we do with our eyes.

Among other things, animals
use hearing to sense danger, like
the sound of a padding wolf or
hissing snake. They use hearing to
find food, like scuttling mice and
buzzing insects. They use hearing to find friends and
mates, by listening for froggy croaks, cricket chirps
and twittering birdsongs. Some use their hearing to
find their way across huge oceans, plains and deserts.
What's more, hearing allows animals to do all this
even in pitch darkness, when there's no light available
for seeing.

For this reason, hearing is often the most
important sense for **nocturnal animals** – animals
that live, hunt and scamper by night. Of course, a
few billion two-legged mammals use their ears in
other ways too. We humans use them to chat, sing,
create music, and listen to Internet radio.

How do ears work?

Ears work by picking up **sound waves**, which are waves of wobbling pressure created by things that vibrate. Lots of things vibrate, and everything vibrates in a slightly different way. **Guitar strings** vibrate back and forth when they're plucked. **Drum skins** vibrate up and down when they're thumped. **Screeching brakes** vibrate as they rub against wheels. And when we talk, shout and sing, it's the **vibrating vocal cords** in our throats that make the noises we hear.

The first animals to 'hear' things were **fish**. Fish have a line of fluid-filled cells running along each side of their bodies. These work like ears on the surface of the skin, picking up waves and ripples from the water around them. This is why goldfish startle and swim away if you tap on the side of the tank with a finger – the tapping makes the glass vibrate, which sends ripples through the water to the fish's skin. Through these waves, the fish 'hears' the tapping and swims quickly away from it, figuring that most sudden sounds mean 'danger'.

In the journey from the water to land – and from fish to frogs, reptiles and birds – these 'surface' ears became smaller, and eventually moved inside the head to become **'inner' ears.** These are the types of ears found in most mammals, including us.

Inside Your Earholes

Humans, like most other mammals, have three basic parts to their ears:

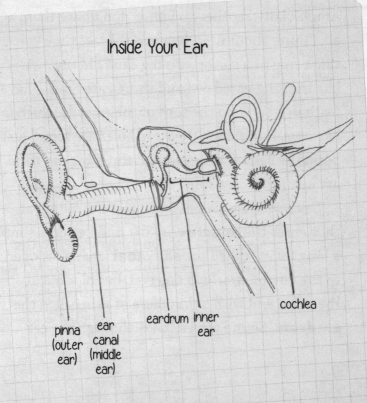

Inside Your Ear

pinna (outer ear)

ear canal (middle ear)

eardrum

inner ear

cochlea

The **outer ear** (or **pinna**) is basically a big, fleshy funnel. It channels sound waves into the earhole (or ear canal) and the eardrum inside, so that it can pick up even weak, faint sounds. When we say someone has 'big ears', the pinna is the bit we're usually talking about. In humans, it's made of cartilage and skin, and shaped a bit like a flat seashell. In other mammals, the pinna may be triangular (as in cats and dogs), circular (as in bears) or long and thin (as in rabbits).

Though you may not have noticed, it's only really mammals that have these outer, visible ears. Amphibians, reptiles and birds don't have them at all. (Think about it – when was the last time you saw a frog or a snake with big ears?) Many owls – like the long-eared owl and short-eared owl – have feathered tufts on the tops of their heads which *look* like ears. But in fact, their ear-holes are found just beside or behind the eyes, and those big ear-tufts are just for decoration.

Once sound waves make it past the outer ear, they enter the **middle ear**. The middle ear is simply a long tube – called the **ear canal** – which is open to the outside world at one end, but blocked at the other end with a thin piece of skin called the **eardrum**. Sound waves ripple through the ear canal and bounce off the eardrum, making it wobble and vibrate in time. Mammals tend to have long ear canals, while reptiles and amphibians have very short ones, or no middle ear at all! **Frogs**, for example, have their eardrums right on the surface of their skins. You can see them as a patch of coloured skin, just beside their eyes.

frog's ear

Behind the human eardrum lie the bones, spaces and organs of the **inner ear**. These are the things you actually hear with. All the other bits just channel wobbling sound waves towards the eardrum. With this job done, the wobbling eardrum transfers its movement into three tiny bones attached to the back of it, which in turn pass vibrations to the **cochlea**.

The **cochlea** is a long tube filled with hairs and gooey fluid, all coiled up into a snail-like shell shape. This is the end of the road for the sound waves. As they vibrate through the watery coils of the cochlea, they contact the thousands of tiny hairs that lie inside. These hairs bend and sway like long grasses in the wind, and send nerve signals to the brain in time with their rippling movements. It's *these* signals that the brain recognizes as sounds. In the end, every sound we hear gets turned into nerve signals in the brain – whether it's a guitar chord, a lion's roar, or Justin Bieber hitting a squeaky high note.

But because animal ears and brains are all different, not all animals hear the same sounds. Many have far better hearing than we do, while others can hardly hear at all. *Some can even 'see' with their **ears**.* Don't believe me? Then read on . . .

Do dogs hear better than we do?

It's *not just dogs* that hear better than humans. In fact, *most* animals have better hearing than we do – including **cats**, **mice**, **dolphins** and **moths**!

Humans, gorillas, chimps and other members of the ape family rely more on their eyesight than their hearing. But for many animals, it's the other way around. Without their keen sense of hearing, most birds, insects, leopards, wolves, bats, sea lions and killer whales would be unable to find their food, avoid their predators, or survive in the big, bad world.

Is it because they have bigger ears?

Having big, triangular ears like a **fox**, **wolf** or **serval cat** *does* help to funnel more sound into the ear, and helps 'big-eared' animals pick out quieter sounds. And besides hearing lower-volume sounds, many animals can also *hear sounds that we can't*, because their ears can pick up higher or lower **pitches** of sound than ours can.

Remember when we said that sounds are made by things that vibrate, which create waves or wobbles of pressure in the air? Well, the **volume** (or loudness) of the sound depends on how much the thing is vibrating, while the **pitch** – how deep or squeaky the sound is – depends on how fast it's vibrating.

Try for yourself:

o Hold a plastic ruler over the edge of a table, and twang the free end. This makes the ruler **vibrate**, which in turn makes the air vibrate around it, creating **sound waves**.

o If you twang the ruler a bit **harder**, it makes

53

bigger waves in the air, which can travel further before they run out.

So the **volume** (or loudness) of a sound depends on how **wide and powerful** the vibration is. **Volume** is measured in **Decibels (Db)**.

o   Now try shortening and lengthening the free end of the ruler by sliding it back and forth as you twang the free end.

o   When there's *less* ruler to twang, the sound gets **higher**. This is because it is now vibrating **more quickly** – waving up and down **more times per second**. But when you make the free end longer, the sound gets **lower**. This is because the ruler is now vibrating **more slowly**, flapping up and down **fewer times per second**, compared with before.

So the **pitch** of a sound (or how high or low the sound is) depends on **how many times per second** the object is vibrating. **Pitch** is measured in **sound waves per second,** or **Hertz (Hz)**.

Now we understand how volume and pitch work, we can understand how the ears of other animals – like cats, bats, dogs and whales – differ from ours . . .

ANIMAL SENSE

Secret Sounds and Super-ears

There are **two** main reasons why many animals can hear sounds we can't.

Firstly, their ears are often more sensitive to fainter sound waves, caused by smaller movements and vibrations. Humans can't hear the beating wings of a moth, because their movement is so small and soft that they create tiny, weak sound *'Sssshhh'* waves in the air – sound waves too small and weak for our eardrums to pick up. But we can all hear the sound of a gunshot, because a bullet exploding out of a gun creates huge waves of pressure in the air, which hit our ears hard and force the eardrums and bones and hairs of the inner ear to vibrate very hard. (In fact, if you're too close, they can wobble so hard that they're permanently damaged, leaving you unable to hear much at all.)

Humans can easily hear sounds ranging from **1 decibel** (raindrops falling on grass) right up to

140 decibels (gunshots and fireworks) and above. Anything above 100 decibels can damage your ears if you hear it for long enough – which is why you should keep your iPod turned down a bit!

Second, other animals have ears that are sensitive to **pitches** (or **frequencies**) of sound that the human ear cannot pick up. **Cat** and **dog ears** can hear squeaky sounds that are **2 or 3 times higher pitched** than the highest sound we can hear. **Dolphin**, **bat** and **moth ears** can hear sounds at pitches **50–100 times higher**. This super-high-pitched sound is called ultrasound, and we'll see later on how some animals can use it like radar, to detect each other in complete darkness.

On the flipside, **African elephants** can hear sounds that are too deep (or low-pitched) for humans to hear, called **infrasound**. When they hear the rumble of a distant thunderstorm across the dry plains of Africa, they walk towards it, looking for rain and fresh water. They also use low, rumbling calls to talk to each other across distances of 4 miles (6km) or more.

Different ear-sensitivity gives different animals very different ranges of hearing. Check out the list of hearing ranges below. Each one is measured in Hertz, or sound waves per second.

Animal Hearing Ranges

200 to 150,000 Hz
moth

1,000 to 240,000 Hz
dolphin

1,000 to 100,000 Hz
mouse

100 to 40,000 Hz
sea lion

100 to 60,000 Hz
cat

50 to 12,000 Hz
pigeon

20 to 20,000 Hz
young adult human

50 to 8,000 Hz
elderly human

1 to 20,000 Hz
elephant

5 to 2,000 Hz
goldfish

Do snakes have ears?

Snakes don't have ears, but that doesn't mean they can't hear things . . .

Most **reptiles** – like lizards and geckos – lack floppy or 'sticky-outy' external ears like mammals. Instead, their eardrums can be seen right on the surface of their heads, just as they can in frogs. In fact, if you hold a lizard still and shine a light on to the thin skin of its eardrum, you can partly see through it, and spot bits of its jawbone moving about underneath.

Most **lizards** hear sounds **between 500 and 4,000 Hz**. This means their hearing isn't quite as good as that of humans and other mammals.

Lizards have trouble hearing low-pitched sounds, but can pick out squealing car tyres or hissing snakes fairly well. So if you want to talk to a gecko, you're best off making squeaky chirping sounds, like a bird. (I tried this once in Thailand, and spent *squeak!* *squeak!* about an hour exchanging squeaks with a gecko on my wall!) *squeak!* *squeak!* *squeak!*

Snakes, however, have no eardrums, no earholes, and no external ears at all. But that doesn't mean they're completely deaf. In fact, many snakes can hear pretty well and, in certain ranges, they hear better than cats! But how?

Legless Lizards

Well, **snakes** (along with **skinks** and other **burrowing lizards**) evolved from lizard-like reptiles with legs and eardrums. But as they spent more time swimming and burrowing through dirt, sand, water and thick undergrowth, they became more streamlined. They lost their legs, and scaly skin grew over their delicate earholes and eardrums to protect them from damage. But although their external ears disappeared beneath the skin, they still kept the inner ears inside their skulls.

This is what allows an 'earless' snake to hear the footsteps of a passing human. Instead of picking up vibrations in the air, through their eardrums, snakes pick up vibrations from the ground, using their bellies and jawbones.

It's a bit like putting your ear to the wall to listen to a conversation in the next room. Low-pitched sounds (or vibrations) travel fairly well through solid earth. If the snake wants to listen hard, it places the sensitive lower edge of its jaw on the ground, and vibrations rumble up from the ground, along its jaw, and into the snake's inner ears. Otherwise, it just picks up sounds through the ribs of its belly as it slithers and crawls. These vibrations pass from the ground, through the snake's ribs, and up along the spine to the skull and inner ears.

Using jawbone/belly hearing, snakes can hear well enough to hear someone talking quietly **up to 10 feet away**. Although they'd have trouble figuring out how high up the person's mouth was (or where, exactly, the sound came from), they'd still have an idea of which direction – north, south, east or west – the sound came from, and slither stealthily in the opposite direction.

Crocodile ears?

Crocodiles, **alligators** and **turtles** do have external ears. Unlike lizards, they can hear deep, low-frequency sounds pretty well, but aren't so sharp with higher-pitched squeaks and squeals. This is because they live (mostly) underwater, where low-pitched sounds can travel long distances, but high-pitched sound waves quickly break up. Out of the water, turtles and crocodiles communicate with high-pitched hisses, but underwater crocodiles, at least, prefer low-pitched rumbles.

Crocodiles also have a rather neat trick for protecting their ears underwater. They have a movable flap of skin lying over their earholes, which they can close up at will, reducing the ear to a narrow slit when they submerge. It's like *they have earlids instead of eyelids*! To keep their underwater hearing ability sharp, some crocodiles also have little pits in their faces and bodies that are especially sensitive to underwater sounds and pressure changes. So in a way, *they have ears all over their bodies*!

Why do birds sing?

Animals with great hearing also tend to be great **talkers and singers**. This is how most of the world's land animals chat, argue, find their mates, and stake out their territory. And while they might not all talk and sing the way we do, if you know what to listen for, you'll hear animals chatting and singing all over the place.

Male birds sing to attract females and warn other male birds away. Singing louder, faster or more complicated songs tells others that they are fitter and stronger than the rest. So the females pick the best singers, and the other males know not to mess with them.

Young birds learn songs from their parents by listening and copying. So their songs not only differ from birds of other species, they also have 'family' songs that are passed down between generations. To us, the song of a **skylark** sounds different to that of a **mistle thrush**. But mistle thrushes can hear the difference between *each other's* songs too. It's like having a family song for each mistle-thrush clan, which every thrush can recognize, and think 'Ooh, that's the Smiths, the Murphys or the McDonalds!'

Believe it or not, **frogs have songs** too. While some frogs only croak and grunt, others **chime** like bells, **whistle** like flutes, and **rumble** like lorries rolling over bridges!

Again, it's the **males that sing loudest** – although female frogs often sing back, in softer voices. Many frogs have huge pouches in their throats that swell with air, and then blast out of their mouths to create *incredibly* loud croaks, whistles and rumbles. In the rainforests of South America, the sound of millions of tree frogs all singing together each night can be deafening.

Many insects, like **crickets**, **grasshoppers** and **cicadas**, have their own songs and mating calls too. Many create **buzzes**, **chirps** and **hissing noises** by rubbing their wings together, or rubbing their legs against their bodies.

Cats, **dogs** and **other mammals** 'sing' too. Large **wolf packs** howl their songs loudly to warn off other packs, while **New Guinea singing dogs** live

alone, and sing to warn other dogs off their patch of forest. Male **lions** roar to warn other prides away, while male **tigers** roar to attract females or threaten other males. **Whales** and **dolphins** sing to each other beneath the waves, and by night, **mice**, **rats** and **bats** sing to each other in squeaky sounds too high-pitched for our human ears to pick up.

Scientists are only just beginning to understand how and why animals talk, sing and communicate. But one thing's for certain – having good hearing seems to make all animals chatty!

BIG SENSE

Which animal has the biggest ears?

Compared to their body size, bats have some of the largest (or rather, longest) ears around. The **brown long-eared bat** was named for its lengthy lugs, and although its huge ears allow it to hear squeaking insects and the echoes of its own ultrasonic screams, they are also pretty slow flyers, as their *ears create drag in the wind*! The Spotted Bat has longer ears still. At **5cm (2 inches) in length**, its ears are almost *two-thirds* the size of its 8cm (3-inch) body. If a human had ears that big, they would stick up 2 feet, making them 8 feet tall!

Many desert mammals have large ears too. With its long tail and springing back legs, the **long-eared jerboa** looks like a cross between a gerbil and a tiny kangaroo. Its huge ears help it to lose heat and stay cool – a bit like having a *sun-roof* in your car. The **fennec fox** is the smallest member of the fox family, but has the **largest ears of any carnivore**. Its 15cm (6-inch) ears make up almost half its height when sticking straight up. Like jerboas, they use their huge ears to stay cool, but also to listen for insects scuttling beneath the desert sands.

Rabbits, of course, take home some prizes for their long ears too. **Wild black-tailed jackrabbits** have **huge 17cm (6.5-inch) ears** for keeping cool in the deserts of the southwestern USA. But the longest ears of all belong to pet bunnies bred in captivity. Lop-eared rabbits have been bred for decades for their long, droopy ears. The longest ever measured belong to Nipper's Geronimo, an English lop with a total ear span of 80cm, or nearly 3 feet!

But the overall prize for largest ears goes to the **African elephant**. Their massive ears measure up to **107cm (42 inches) across**. They help the elephant to stay cool by venting heat from their bodies, but they also use them to fan themselves, and to waft their scent over long distances to attract mates.

Which animal has the smallest ears?

Just as many desert animals have big ears for losing heat and staying cool, animals that live in cold, icy climates tend to have small ears. These tiny 'ear vents' release very little heat and help the animal stay warm. Unlike their jackrabbit cousins, **Arctic hares** have short, stubby ears that help them to stay cozy in the frozen plains of the Arctic. **Snow leopards**, which live in the high, snow-capped mountains of Central Asia, have the smallest, stubbiest ears of any big cat. Again, these help the leopards stay warm in freezing temperatures.

Although, they're now extinct, **mammoths** – the woolly cousins of today's big-eared elephants – had the smallest ears in the elephant family. This helped them to survive for thousands of years, at a time when all of North America, Europe and Asia were covered with snow and ice. If our ancestors hadn't hunted them to extinction, they'd still be around today.

So which animal has the smallest ears of all?

A spider, perhaps?

Or an ant?

Well, spiders and insects don't really have ears like ours. As we'll learn later on, they have touch-sensors on their legs and bodies that work a bit like ears instead. The *smallest* animal with ears similar to ours would probably be a **tiny frog**. The **Monte Iberian eleuth frog** is the smallest in the world. It was discovered in the mountains of Cuba in 1996, and measures just 8mm long – little bigger than a garden pea! **It's ears are less than half a millimetre across**, so this little guy probably has the smallest ears on the planet.

Which animal has the best hearing?

Although many birds have around the same range of hearing as humans, some birds have far more powerful hearing at certain pitches, or frequencies, than we do. **Owls** probably have the best *'pinpoint'* or *3D hearing*. Their earholes lie beside their eyes, at slightly

Toowit Toowoo

69

different heights, which helps them pick out the exact source of a faint squeak or chirp and home in on it. **Oilbirds** and **cave swifts** can hear *incredibly high-pitched sounds*, and use *ultrasonic chirps* to navigate in the dark, in much the same way that bats do. (We'll learn more about that in the next section.)

Pigeons, on the other hand, can hear *incredibly low-pitched sounds*, which allows them to hear the rumble of a far-off thunderstorm, or the deep crashing of waves against cliffs many miles away. They use their hearing – along with a special magnetic sense – to find their way home across distances of thousands of miles. Other migrating birds, like **terns** and **albatrosses**, may do the same.

What about **cats** and **dogs**? Which pet has the best ears in your home? Well, although many people think dog ears are better, in fact, cats win the prize. Not only do they have more sensitive hearing, across a wider ranges of pitches (so yes – *cats can hear dog whistles too*), they can also use **30 muscles in each ear to rotate their ears through 180 degrees**, helping them to focus

in on sounds more quickly than dogs can. That's why dogs tilt and swivel their heads when they hear something, while cats simply turn a lazy ear toward it.

Which animal has the worst hearing?

Many primitive animals like **sponges**, **worms**, **clams** and **jellyfish** have *no* hearing organs at all, so live *silent lives* beneath the earth and waves. But of those that can hear, **fish** probably have the poorest sense of hearing. Although a **tuna** can 'hear' underwater sounds ranging from 50 Hz to 1,000 Hz through the pressure-sensing organs in its skin, its hearing is about **20 times weaker than ours**. So if you're out fishing, I wouldn't worry too much about scaring the fish away by singing or talking. They can hear boat engines well enough, but not people chatting at the surface.

Although most moggies and mongrels have great hearing, some **pure-bred, pedigree cats** and **dogs** can be born deaf or partially deaf due to inbreeding. **Siamese, White Persian** and **Turkish Angora cats** are often born with deafness or hearing problems. Among dog breeds, 1 in 10 **Dalmatians** is born deaf in both ears, while 1 in 5 is deaf in one ear. Other hard-of-hearing pooches include **bull terriers, cocker spaniels**, and **Jack Russells**.

What's the loudest animal in the world?

Since so many of the world's animals use sound to communicate long-distance, there are plenty of animals in the running for the title of 'world's loudest animal'.

Howling wolves and **roaring lions** can be heard 5–10 miles away.

Humans can't hear the low, rumbling noises made by **elephants**, but they're actually incredibly loud, and can travel over 20 miles between herds.

The whoops and roars of **howler monkeys** can travel 20 miles through dense forest, and reach an ear-splitting 90 decibels (human shouting only reaches about 70).

Bullfrogs and **cicadas** are incredibly loud (over

100 decibels) at close range, but their high-pitched sounds tend to tail off quickly over distance.

The very loudest animal noises are made underwater. **Blue whales** croon and whistle to each other over distances of hundreds of miles, and their booming songs can reach an incredible 188 decibels. That's louder than a jet engine at a distance of 10 feet. Yet even they don't take the 'loudest animal' prize.

The title actually goes to the **pistol shrimp** – the gangster of the underwater world. The pistol shrimp is a small crustacean that lives in the deep sea, and it earns its name from the gun-like bangs it creates with its snapping claws. It snaps its claws together with such speed and ferocity that – over very short, underwater distances – the sound hits over 200 decibels, making it sound like a gunshot or a massive, underwater explosion. The sound is so powerful that it kills small fish that get too close to it. Which is, of course, why the shrimp lets rip with the bang in the first place.

World's Loudest Animal

SPECIAL SENSE

Do bats have radar?

No, they don't. But they do *use their incredible ears a bit like radar dishes* – using them to spot their prey in the dark, just as navy captains use radar to spot enemy ships at sea.

The difference is in the waves that bounce back and forth between the hunter and the hunted. While a ship's radar sends and receives radio waves, bats send and receive sound waves. They shout and scream into the darkness, then listen for the echoes that bounce back. Incredibly, many bats' ears are so sensitive and so finely tuned that they can use these echoes to pinpoint everything from frogs and crickets to moths and mosquitoes. This is called **echolocation** – literally, finding things with echoes.

Hunting with sound

Here's how it works.

First, the bat creates a **pulse of sound waves** by making an **ultra-high-pitched shriek**. These sound waves travel forward from the bat's head as waves of pressure in the air. Eventually, they reach an object – either a non-moving obstacle like a tree, or a moving target like a moth. When the sound waves strike the object, they bounce off it, and some are bounced back toward the bat, as **echoes**.

Now here's the clever bit. **Bigger targets** (like fat moths) **reflect *more* sound waves than small targets** (like mosquitos). So the bat can tell *how big the target is* from the volume of the echoes that reach its ears. And just as owls can pinpoint a squeaking mouse by listening, bats can also pinpoint the **direction** and **distance** to a target by comparing how long it takes the echoing sound waves to reach each ear.

Most impressively of all, bats can also tell **which direction a target is moving** in, and **how fast**

it is moving. This allows a flying bat to pick a buzzing mosquito out of the air with incredible accuracy. They're the ultimate flying stealth hunters.

What do bat screams sound like?

The squeaky scream of a bat is pitched so high that humans (and *even cats and dogs*) cannot hear it. It lies in the range of sound we call **ultrasound**, and if we could hear it, it would sound like a series of high-pitched clicks – a bit like the noise it makes when you get something stuck in the wheels of your bike.

Most bats scream through their mouths. Others, though, scream through their noses through special, horn-like nose-leaf organs that help aim, focus and amplify the sound.

Are bats the only animals that can do this?

Nope – far from it. Some birds, like **oilbirds** and **cave swifts**, use echolocation to navigate the dark caverns where they live. Some dolphins and whales can do it too. **Chinese** and **Ganges River dolphins** use echolocation to find fish in the dark, murky rivers of India and China. **Bowhead whales** use echolocation to find their way around beneath the ice sheets of the Arctic.

Some **shrews** echolocate to navigate and avoid predators too. And although they're nowhere near as good at it as bats, *even* **human beings** can do it if they're forced to practise. Blind and sight-impaired people can become surprisingly good at hearing echoes bouncing off large objects. Some even go biking and mountain-biking, using their ears alone to safely find their way!

A few animals, like some moths, also use clever tactics to 'jam' echolocating hunters. When a tiger moth is approached by a screaming bat, it **screams back in ultrasound**. The scream is so loud that the bat's ears are overwhelmed with noise. Sometimes this startles and stuns the bat so much that it completely loses its bearings, and has to land to avoid crashing into something. At the very least, it jams the bat's ultrasonic radar, so the bat can't zero in on where the moth is and flies past, giving the moth a chance to escape. It's like sound-based aerial warfare. If the moth loses the sound battle, it gets eaten; if the bat loses, it doesn't get to eat.

CHAPTER 3: SMELL

COMMON SENSE

How do dogs smell?

Awful. At least they do
when they're wet.

Ahem. OK – rubbish jokes aside, smell is a pretty
fascinating thing. It's one of the simplest and oldest
animal senses – it appeared long before the more
complex senses of vision and hearing.

In almost all animals, **smell is linked to taste**
(which we'll look at later). In most species these
two senses **work together** to help animals find out
about the world around them. Smell helps all kinds

of animals – from butterflies and beetles to bears and baboons – to find food, find their friends, and steer clear of danger.

What is smell for?

Why would an animal need to smell its way around, when it could just **look** for food and friends, or **listen** for danger instead?

Well, for starters, you can do things with **noses** that you can't do with eyes and ears. If you live in swampy, muddy water or the dark depths of the ocean, it's not so easy to spot the tasty plants you might be looking for. And you certainly can't listen for them, as most plants aren't too chatty. But if the plants give off a smell – either through the air, or through the water – then you can smell your way towards your food quite happily.

Likewise, if you're a small animal living in a dense forest or tall grasses, then you may be pounced upon by a lurking hunter long before you see it. If it's stealthy enough, you might not hear it, either. But since pretty much all animals give off smells and odours (some more than others – I'm looking at you, Mr Skunk), a keen nose might help you smell that stalking cat, wolf or weasel long before it gets close enough to bite you.

Plus, as we've already discovered, *not all animals can see and hear*. Eyes and ears are quite complex organs, and it took a while (at least a few billion years) for living things to evolve them. So smell was how most living things found food for the billions of years *before* the other senses came along. And for most living things, it's still the main way they find food, even today. In short, most **life on Earth follows its nose**.

Why do flowers, cheese and poo smell different?

Smell is basically all about **chemicals**. When you hear the word chemicals, you probably think of stinky liquids in a school chemistry lab, or perhaps the stinky liquids we use to clean our houses and clothes, like bleach and washing powder. But pretty much everything you see around you is a chemical.

A chemical is any substance — solid, liquid or gas — that is made using chemical reactions between atoms and molecules.

Air is a chemical – it's a mixture of oxygen, nitrogen and other chemical elements.

Seawater is a chemical – it's a mixture of hydrogen, oxygen, sodium and whatever else is dissolved in it.

Even **wood, bone and blood are chemicals** – made up of differing amounts of carbon, hydrogen, oxygen and other chemical elements.

Now here's the clever bit. Pretty much every chemical substance on the planet is **slowly crumbling or dissolving into the air or water** around it.

Wooden chairs smell 'woody' because they release tiny amounts of wood-smelling chemicals into the air around them. Similarly, **roses** smell like roses because they release sweet, rose-smelling chemicals into the air (in fact, they do this on purpose, so that insects can find them and pollinate them). And **dog poo** smells like dog poo because . . . well, you get the idea.

Often, these chemicals take the form of liquids (like blood, sweat or urine) released from animal bodies. A brown bear, for example, can detect the stinky sweat of a human – carried in tiny droplets on the wind – from over a mile away.

But plants, fungi and other living things give off smells too. Seaweeds give off weedy smells underwater, making them easier for manatees and marine iguanas to find. On land, groundnuts, mushrooms and truffles release stinky substances into the soil, so that wild pigs and other animals can find them even if they're buried beneath the ground.

Almost every chemical substance on earth gives off its own particular smell, and if our noses were sensitive enough, we could smell them all.

What gets up your nose?

Cat hairs?
Bogeys?
Bits of pollen
that make you sneeze?

All sorts of things get up our noses every day. But what happens to them once they're up there, and why do some things have strong, memorable smells, while other things don't?

Smell is all about sensing chemicals. When an animal smells something, it is actually sensing a tiny amount of a chemical in the air or water around it.

To recognize a smell, two things have to happen.

First, the animal's nose (or whatever it smells with) has to detect the chemical. This part is quite simple. Basically, the chemical is sucked into the nostrils, where it meets a layer of special smelling cells (or **olfactory cells**) lining the nose. These cells contain thousands of chemical-sensing proteins, called **chemoreceptors**. When the right chemical contacts the right receptor, it sends a message to the brain to confirm that a certain chemical has been detected.

Now comes the **second** part. The message is passed through nerves to the bit of the brain called the smell centre (or **olfactory bulb**).

That Smell Rings a Bell . . .

Inside the smell centre, the brain compares this 'smell signal' with others it has received in the past. If the brain finds a match, then the animal will recognize the smell. If there's no match, then the brain creates a new smell memory, and stores it for future use.

Humans, of course, attach **words** to these smells – words like '**strawberry**', '**sweaty sock**' or '**dog poo**'.

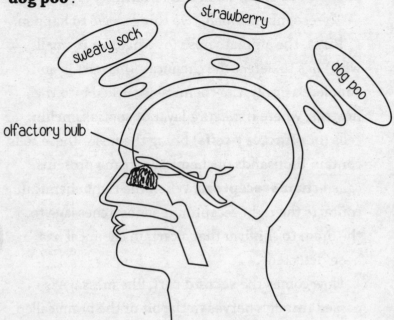

Other animals just remember them as feelings – the way we would remember the vague smell of our grandmother's house, or the air after a rainstorm.

Most animals have a better sense of smell than humans, as they have more (and more different types of) smell-sensors, and more of their brains devoted to smell. The olfactory bulb (smell centre) in a **brown bear**'s brain, for example, is **five times larger** than the average human's. Which is why they can detect food smells up to 20 miles away, while some of us have trouble smelling our own B.O.

Why do we love some smells, but hate others?

Different things smell good and bad to different animals. A **dung beetle**, for example, may love the smell of
dung, while **bees** love the
smell of **flowers**, and

humans love the smell of **cherries**, **chocolate** and
cheeseburgers.

This isn't so surprising, perhaps, if you remember what smell is (mostly) for –
finding food. Bees and butterflies like the sweet smell of flowers because they hint at the lovely, sweet, sugary nectar waiting for them inside. Humans like the smell of cherries and cheeseburgers for similar reasons – it hints at the delicious, sugary, fatty or meaty goodness trapped inside the food. And dung beetles, well . . . each to their own, I suppose.

The point is, **all animals need to eat**, and **smells help us to find foods** that will (for the most part, anyway) be good for us, and help build our bodies.

Smells Like . . . Sick

So if that's the case, then why do some smells – like rotten eggs, sour milk and dog poo – put us off, or even make us feel sick? Well, just as 'nice' smells help us to find 'good' food, 'bad' smells help us to avoid 'bad' foods. **Old, rotten eggs** smell bad because they are riddled with **bacteria**, which

release the (poisonous) gas **sulphur dioxide** as they grow inside the egg. The same goes for **sour milk**, which curdles as bacteria grow in it, feasting on the sugars inside. If we ate a rotten egg or drank a glass of 'off' milk, we'd swallow the bacteria and get sick. So the smell puts us off, and stops us from eating dodgy foods.

If a food has made us sick **before**, then the *memory* of its smell may even trigger a feeling of being sick, warning us of what's to come. And although we're not likely to eat or drink them any time soon, the same thing applies to **dog poo**, **murky pond water** and **open sewers**. Their **terrible smells** warn us that nasty bacteria or other nasties are lurking inside, so they're probably best avoided.

Of course, following smell trails to tasty foods isn't the only use for a good nose. That may have been the original use for the sense of smell, but while most animals still use it that way, many also use their smelly-sense to **avoid predators**, **find their mates and families**, **mark their territory** and **navigate** the land, sea and sky.

ANIMAL SENSE

How do sharks smell blood underwater?

When we think of smell, we usually think of heady scents wafting through the air. But some smells and odours can travel through water and other liquids too. It all depends on whether or not the chemical that causes the smell (whether it's blood, bleach or bird poo) can dissolve in water. If it does, then **the chemicals are carried on ocean and river currents** just as airy scents are carried on the breeze.

If it doesn't, then the stinky chemical will either stay at the surface, sink to the bottom, or stay suspended in the water close to where it was released, making it difficult or impossible for marine animals to smell them at a distance.

Smells Fishy

Since smell was one of the first senses to develop, **most fish have noses** (or rather, smelling organs).

But since they don't breathe air like land animals, their noses work a bit differently to ours.

Humans and other land animals smell the same air they breathe, as it makes its way from the nose to the lungs. Fish, on the other hand, breathe by passing water through their gills. But since their nostrils (actually, nose-holes are called **nares** in fish) don't lead to their gills, they can't sniff at the water as it flows through. Their noses are like pits, bowls, or dead-ends. So they don't really 'suck' or 'sniff' water into them to smell things. Instead, **water just flows in and out from the sea or river around them**. From there, the water passes over their olfactory cells lying within the nares, which bind certain chemicals and send 'smell signals' to the brain, just as our noses do.

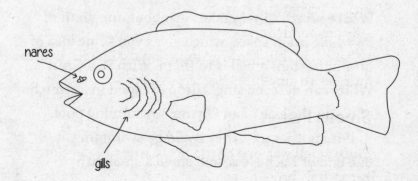

nares

gills

Some fish – like **freshwater pike** and **carp** – have poorly developed noses, and can barely smell a worm dangling right in front of them. But others – like **sharks**, **rays** and **eels** – have a powerful sense of underwater smell, and use it to hunt other animals beneath the waves.

Sniffer Sharks

Sharks, in particular, are masterful underwater smell detectors. Sharks eat more or less everything, including fish, crabs, lobsters, turtles, plankton, shellfish, seals and other sharks. (They also – very occasionally – take bites out of human swimmers, surfers and scuba divers. But they don't like the taste of us much, and tend to let go once they figure out we're not funny-looking seals.)

The olfactory bulb (or smell centre) in a **Great White shark**'s brain takes up about one-sixth of its whole brain space, which gives you some idea of how important smell is to them. With it, a Great White can detect a single drop of blood in a stretch of ocean the size of an Olympic swimming pool.

Put another way, they could be swimming at one end of Loch Ness, and smell a small fish swimming away at the other.

Not that there *are* any Great White sharks in Loch Ness, of course.

Loch Ness is a **freshwater lake**, and Great Whites can only survive in **saltwater seas** and oceans.

Besides – the **monster** would have scoffed them all, right?

It's thought that Great Whites also use their noses to **migrate** and **find each other**, scenting changes in ocean scents and special signalling chemicals called **pheromones** in the water. They also have the rather frightening habit of lifting their heads several feet out of the water. Terrified sailors used to think they did this to get a better look at them in their boats. But we now know that they're really **lifting their noses** (rather than their eyes) high into the air to catch the scents of **distant seal colonies** and **whale carcasses**. No less scary if you're a seal, perhaps . . .

Smell signs

It's not just sharks that use smelly chemicals to hunt, find mates and find their way about. Many other animals use pheromones and other smell-signals too.

Wolves and **dogs**, quite famously, like to pee on things to mark out their territory. But in fact, most mammals – including **cats**, **mice**, **bears**, **lemurs**, **monkeys**, **chimps**, **elephants** and **hippos** use their smelly urine or poo to mark out their territory too. Some animals, like **lions** and **leopards** – just pee on the ground to mark the edge of their land. Others, like **lemurs**, pee on their own hands and feet, and leave smelly hand and footprints wherever they go. In any case, the message is clear to everyone who smells it: 'Keep out', 'This is mine' or 'Go away . . . or else'.

Insects use smell signals too, using their antennae to pick up chemical trails from the ground, air or water. **Ants** leave smell trails for each other towards new sources of food, like Hansel and Gretel dropping breadcrumbs in the forest. When one ant finds a piece of rotting fruit, or a tasty bird carcass, it leaves a scent trail all the way back to the nest, so that the other ants can follow it straight to the grub, and bring it back in lots of tiny pieces. This is why you see lines of busy ants weaving around objects and up and down walls and tree trunks – they're all following a smell trail to or from the nest.

Do ants have noses?

No, they don't. But that doesn't mean they can't smell. Noses are just big, handy organs of smell. But lots of animals sniff their way around without them, as their chemical-sensing chemoreceptors are found elsewhere. **Fruit flies**, for example, have their smell-sensors on their **legs** – so in a way, they smell things through their *feet*! Many simple animals like **flatworms** have smell-sensors on their **skin**. This allows them to absorb smells from the soil or water around them and wriggle toward food sources they couldn't otherwise find.

   Ants, moths and other **insects** pick up scent trails from the air with their **feathery antennae**. Incredibly, moths can tell as much about each other from their airy scents as dogs can from their friendly bottom-sniffing. During the moth mating season, female moths release massive **pheromone plumes** – nice-smelling *stinkbombs* – which travel for miles across fields and forests. Using their antennae, male moths follow these perfumed trails to find their true love. When the males arrive, the females weigh them up based on the male pheromones *they* give off. With a quick fly-by and a waft of their antennae, the females can tell how old a male is, which family he's from, and how good a father he's likely to be.

Many biologists believe that human females do this too. So the message is clear for stinky boys – as far as girls are concerned, **B.O. is a no-no**.

Time to hit the showers, lads . . .

BIG SENSE

Which animal has the largest nose?

Male **proboscis monkeys**, which live in the forests of Borneo, are famous for their enormous, dangly noses. In females, the nose looks pretty normal. But in males, it grows to a length of **18cm (7 inches)** or more, and looks like a big, droopy balloon hanging down over the mouth.

Some **seals** are pretty hefty in the schnozz department too. Named after its land-dwelling nose-a-like, the enormous **northern elephant seal** weighs up to three tons (2,700 kg), and has an inflatable, trunk-like nose around a **foot (30cm)** long.

Elephants, of course, have the longest noses of any animal. The trunk of a fully grown **African elephant** is actually a combination of its nose and upper lip, and can reach over **7 feet (2.1m)** in length.

But the prize for largest 'nose' probably goes to

one of its ocean-going cousins.

The nose of a **sperm whale** takes up about a third of its entire body size, and since adult sperm whales reach sizes of over 60 feet (20m), that means its nose is over **20 feet (7m)** wide! Most of the space is taken up by its huge,

oil-filled spermaceti organ, which it uses to adjust its buoyancy in the water, and to create powerful clicking sounds that work like sonar.

Which animal has the tiniest nose?

Insects, as we've already seen, don't really have noses. They use their antennae to smell things instead – so they're out of the running for this competition. Among birds, the least 'beaky' is probably the **bee hummingbird**, which has a total body length of just **2 inches (5cm)**, and tiny, hair-like nasal passages set into its miniature beak. The most sub-nosed mammal is probably the tiny **hog-nosed (or bumblebee) bat**. At 1.1 inches

(30mm) in length, it's smaller even than the bee hummingbird, and its tiny, pig-like snout is **less than a millimetre wide**, and sits flat on its face.

Which animal has the best sense of smell?

As we've already seen, many **sharks** have an incredible sense of smell – powerful enough to sniff a tiny drop of blood in thousands of litres of seawater. Among birds, most prefer to use sound and vision over smell, but some migrating seabirds, such as **albatrosses**, have keen noses inside their beaks for sniffing out floating food in the dark. On land, **mice** and **rats** are pretty keen sniffers (which is why you shouldn't leave cheese or biscuit crumbs on your kitchen floor – they'll whiff them from outside your house), and some have even been trained to sniff out explosives and landmines for the army!

   Dogs, of course, have an amazing sense of smell.

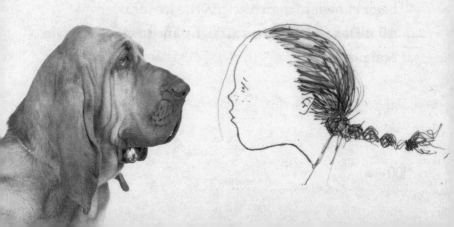

The olfactory region in a human nose (the surface that detects the smelly chemicals) is about the size of a postage stamp, and contains 5 million olfactory (or 'sniffer') cells. In a **bloodhound**, it's about the size of a handkerchief, and contains over **230 million sniffer cells**. This allows them to pick up scents that are weeks, months, or even years old, and follow them for miles.

But the champion sniffer prize actually goes to their carnivore cousins – the **bears**.

Bears have the **most acute sense of smell in the world**, thought to be up to **seven times more powerful than that of dogs**. Over a third of their brains are devoted to smelling things, and they can sniff out food, other predators or each other over enormous distances.

Brown bears can pick up the scent of deer up to **18 miles (30 km)** away, while **polar bears** have been known to march across the ice for over **40 miles (64 km)** in a straight line towards a single seal pup.

Which animal has the worst sense of smell?

Incredibly, compared to our overall brain size, the brains of **humans** have the **smallest olfactory bulb** (or smell centre) of any land animal. Which is one reason why we're so rubbish at smelling things, and tend to depend more on our eyes. In the oceans, **dolphins**, **killer whales** and **sperm whales** have **no smell centres** in their brains, so (as far as we know) have absolutely no sense of smell. Recently, though, biologists have discovered that some whales, like the **bowhead whale**, do have smell centres in their brains. They probably use them to sniff out shoals of krill underwater, which (apparently) smell like rotten, fishy garbage.

Which animal uses its nose most?

Probosicis monkeys and **elephant seals** use their noses like trumpets. Their long, saggy noses straighten out as they blast air through them, making loud hooting and honking sounds to attract females and scare off other males. Boar-like **tapirs**, which live in the rainforests of Brazil and Malaya, have a pretty unique use for their noses too. Tapirs are natural **snorkellers**. When alarmed, they dive into rivers and hide beneath the surface, keeping only their trunk-like noses above the surface for air.

But the prize for most useful nose almost certainly has to go to the elephants. **African** and **Asiatic elephants** use their 'handy' noses like **trumpets**, **snorkels**, **drinking straws**, **shower heads** and more. With their long, muscular trunks, they can trumpet greetings and alarm calls, and snorkel as they swim across rivers (yes, elephants can swim). They also suck water through them like huge drinking straws, and blast it back out again to shower themselves off (or to hose down a grubby friend, like a big, elephant car wash). They also use their trunks to vacuum up bits of food, and – as we'll learn in the Touch chapter – they're also strong, flexible and sensitive enough to be used like our arms, hands or fingers.

Now that's a *prize nose*, if ever I saw one.

Most
Useful
Nose

SPECIAL SENSE

Why do dogs have wet noses?

A dog's cold, wet nose is kept moist with **mucus** squeezed from glands inside the nose. Tiny amounts of smelly chemicals floating in the air then stick to its nose and dissolve into the mucus. As the dog inhales through its nose (with quick bursts of doggie sniffing), it draws these chemicals deep into its nose and into contact with the millions and millions of chemical sensors inside. From there, smell signals are passed to the highly developed olfactory bulb in the dog's brain, where millions of smell-related memories are compared and recognized.

With all this amazing nasal equipment, the average mutt can smell traces of **urine on a lamp post** left by another dog over a year ago. It can smell a week-old **human fingerprint left on a drinking glass**. And some dogs – like bloodhounds and highly trained sniffer dogs – can smell tiny traces of **gunpowder**, **drugs** and **explosives** even inside air-tight plastic containers, and smell **people trapped under several feet of snow, rock or rubble**.

How do sniffer dogs find people?

Most dogs can identify *any* human being by smell, simply by scenting the invisible cloud of skin cells and sweat droplets that we shed from our bodies every hour of every day. No matter how clean we think we are, all of us shed our stinky scents into the air as we move around. To a dog, **every human has a unique smell** – even identical twins – and it's fairly simple to follow the trail of skin cells and sweat drops to their owner. Depending on how keen the dog's nose is, and how much practice it gets, some can follow these **scent trails** for **miles through dense forest**. Even in **crowded cities**, where scent trails from thousands of people become mingled and confused, well-trained sniffer dogs can still follow a single human trail over short distances.

It's not just humans that drop their scent everywhere, either. Birds, rodents, cats, horses,

deer . . . every animal gives off some kind of smell, and leaves some kind of chemical trail for a keen-nosed dog to follow. This is why dogs are so good at tracking and hunting. From the strength of the scent, a dog can tell how long it has been since an animal passed by. If it stopped to pee or poo, the dog can tell what the animal ate recently, whether it's male or female, how old or young it is, and whether it's sick or healthy. And of course, dogs use these scent signals to find out about each other too.

Why do dogs sniff each other's bottoms?

With such a sensitive nose, it's hard to see why the first thing one dog does when it meets another one is to sniff its bottom. But in fact, this is just about the quickest way a dog can get to know somebody new. A dog's main **scent glands** are found in its **bottom**, and dogs can tell all kinds of things about each other from taking a quick whiff. They can tell if the dog is a local, whether it has been around this area before, and whose family (or pack) it belongs to. They can tell if the dog is male, female, or interested in finding a mate. They can tell how the other dog feels about them – whether they're friendly, frightened, stressed or angry.

So dogs don't just use smell to find things. They use smell to **communicate**. They use smell to **listen**, **talk**, **learn** and **remember**. To a dog, the outside world is like a library, a television and an Internet chat-room all rolled into one. Every **lamp post** tells a hundred stories, and every **patch of grass** holds a week's worth of doggie conversations.

Now you know why they love their 'walkies' so much!

CHAPTER 4:
TASTE

COMMON SENSE

Why do sprouts and ice cream taste so different?

Because they contain (and give off) different sorts of **chemicals**. The flavour of ice cream comes from the sweet taste of the sugars and cream used to make it, plus the smell of vanilla, strawberries, chocolate, or whatever else it's flavoured with.

The flavour of sprouts, on the other hand, comes from the bitter taste of their cabbage-like leaves, plus the eggy, sulphurous odours that are released when you boil them.

Hang on – aren't taste and flavour the same thing?

Tastes are simple sensations we get from putting food in our mouths. There are only five basic tastes – **sweet**, **salty**, **bitter**, **sour**, and one more called **umami** that we'll learn a bit more about later on.

Flavours, on the other hand, are more complex sensations we get from both our mouths and our noses. Food flavours – like **chocolate**, **strawberry** or **sprout** – come from a *combination of taste and smell*. So just as there are thousands of different smells in the world, there are tens of thousands of unique flavours too. One for every different type of food.

So if your food doesn't smell (or you can't smell it), then it doesn't seem to have a strong flavour of its own. This is why fairly odourless foods like rice and tofu don't seem to taste of much, and why everything seems tasteless when you have a cold, and your nose is bunged up.

This is also why – strictly speaking – chocolate doesn't really have a taste, other than 'sweet'. But it does have a flavour, which we recognize when we both smell and taste it. Likewise, sprouts don't seem half as bad if you hold your nose when you eat them. Without the eggy smell going up your nose, all your tongue tastes is 'bitter'.

How do tongues taste things?

Just as noses sense chemicals that float in the air, **tongues sense chemicals** on the **surface of your food**. (Or, for that matter, anything else you put in your mouth. After all, rubber car tyres and wooden chair legs have a flavour too!)

What's more, noses and tongues work in similar ways, using special cells containing chemical-sensing proteins (or **chemoreceptors**). In your nose, these recognize certain 'smelly chemicals' and pass messages to a 'smell centre' in the brain. In your **mouth**, they recognize 'tasty chemicals' – like **sweet-tasting sugars** and **bitter-tasting acids** – and pass messages to a **'taste centre'** in the brain instead.

The things that do the actual tasting are called **taste buds**. These are tiny taste organs that line the surface of your tongue, the roof of your mouth (or palate), and the back of your throat. Each taste bud is made up of **50–150 taste cells**, squashed together into a shape something like a tiny grapefruit or orange. It's these taste cells that contain the taste-sensors, which bind and recognize tasty chemicals and relay messages to the brain.

Each taste cell is built to recognize chemicals that relate to one of the five basic tastes. Taste cells that recognize **sugars** like glucose (found in chocolate) and fructose (found in most fruits) send signals to the brain that say '**sweet**'. Cells that recognize **salts** like sodium chloride (aka table salt) and potassium chloride send signals that say – you guessed it – '**salty**'.

But what about the other tastes? Well, '**sour**' signals are sent by taste cells that recognize **certain acids** like acetic acid (found in vinegar) and citric acid (found in lemons). '**Bitter**' signals come from cells that recognize **plant and animal poisons**, plus many other kinds of toxic chemicals (we'll find out why in a minute).

Finally, there are also cells that create the little-known fifth taste sensation – '**umami**' – which you might describe as '**meaty**' or '**savoury**'. This comes from taste cells that recognize some types of **amino acids**, which are the building blocks of **meaty proteins**.

Could you taste things without a tongue?

Yes, you could! Although perhaps not quite as well as with one. This is because taste cells are packed into taste buds that are found not just on your tongue, but *all over your mouth*. In total, you have about **5,000–9,000 taste buds**, with roughly half of them on your tongue, and the other half on your palate, beneath your tongue, and at the back of your throat.

Your tongue, though, contains the *most sensitive* (and the *most different types*) of taste buds, so that's where most of your food-tasting goes on. There, taste buds sit clustered on top of raised bumps on the surface of your tongue called **papillae**. You can see these (the papillae that is, not the taste buds – they're too small to see without a microscope) when you stick your tongue out and look closely at it in the mirror.

The average human has about **250** of these little bumps on their tongue, with 200 papillae at the front (or tip) of the tongue, and the rest at the back and sides. This makes the **tip of your tongue** the most sensitive part for tasting.

Older people have fewer bumps (and taste buds) than younger people, as they tend to disappear as we age (which is maybe one reason why old people actually like eating sprouts!). And other animals may have more or less than this, giving them a more or less powerful sense of taste.

All these papillae contain taste buds that can detect all five of the basic tastes – sweet, salty, sour, bitter and umami. But the different types of taste cells aren't spread evenly across the tongue, so *some* parts of the tongue are *more sensitive* to *specific tastes* than others. The front (or tip) of the tongue is better at sensing sweet. The back of the tongue is better at sensing bitter. And the sides are best at recognizing salty, sour and umami.

bitter
sweet
salty, sour and umami

You can test this out for yourself by dabbing bits of sugar water, salt water or lemon juice on to different parts of your tongue. (Not too much, though, or the mixture of tastes might make you feel a bit sick!)

Why do we taste things?

Firstly, our sense of taste helps us to **identify foods** (like tomatoes and nuts) from non-foods (like pebbles and grass). Sweet and salty-tasting foods contain the sugars and salts we need to help keep us alive, while nutty, meaty foods with savoury (or umami) tastes contain the proteins we need to help us grow. So our craving for foods with certain tastes helps us find the nutrients we need to live.

Secondly – and perhaps most importantly – our sense of taste also helps us to **avoid eating or drinking poisons**, **rotten foods** and other things that might not be good for us. In medieval times, kings often had an official 'food taster', whose job was to eat a little of every meal before the king did – just in case someone had tried to poison it. Well, that's what our tongues and taste buds do for us. They're the guardians at the gates of our mouths, and they help stop nasty things making it through to the stomachs and intestines behind.

Poisonous plants and **animals** create toxic chemicals that taste **bitter**, so a bitter taste warns us not to swallow them. With some very toxic animals, like poison arrow frogs, by the time you've tasted their bitter skin, it's too late. Which is why – as we've already seen in the Sight chapter – they often also display warnings you can see, like bright yellow or orange colouring.

Sour tastes, on the other hand, can warn us if something has '**gone off**', and is swimming with harmful bacteria. Rotten meat and curdled milk both taste sour because they are swarming with bacteria which turn food sugars into sour-tasting acids as they grow.

That's the basics of how and why we taste. But as with sight, hearing and smell, not all animals taste the world the way we do.

Otherwise, how could a dung beetle survive?

Think about it . . .

ANIMAL SENSE

Do cats like chocolate milk?

It's not easy finding out which foods an animal likes. For **humans**, it's simple – we just tell each other about what we've just tasted. **Chimps** and **gorillas**, on the other hand, can't talk. Their facial expressions are a lot like ours, and they grimace and screw up their faces when something tastes bad.

But that only tells us if they really hate something. It's a lot harder to tell whether they really *love* bananas, or whether they think bananas are just OK. And the further away you get on the animal family tree, the harder it is to judge. *You* try guessing whether an ant likes ice cream, or whether a jellyfish likes fish food. After all, when they're hungry enough, *most* animals will eat more or less *anything*.

That said, scientists have found out some things about the tastes of different animals. By offering well-fed animals choices between different foods lots and lots of times, they can tell which foods an animal tends to prefer. And by scanning animals brains while they eat, some scientists have even figured out which foods cats, dogs, rats, rabbits and mice love best. And the answers can be quite surprising. **Cats**, for example, **love milk**. But they're *not bothered* about ***chocolate milk*** at all.

Sour Puss

As it turns out, different animal species **taste things differently**. Just because humans find something sweet, that doesn't mean cat or a cow will think it tastes sweet too. **Cats**, for example, can't detect sweet tastes at all. Unlike humans, the taste buds on a cat's tongue contain no sugar-binding 'sweet detectors'. So to them, chocolate milk tastes like slightly strange or 'off' milk, and a chocolate bar tastes like a lump of solid butter.

On the other hand, cats' tongues *do* have very sensitive detectors for bitter, sour and savoury tastes. This helps explain why cats seem so picky about their food. They *hate* sour things like lime and lemon juice, but *love* savoury, meaty things like beef, chicken, cheese and tuna fish. If they're forced to (by, say, a vegetarian owner) cats *will* eat fruits and vegetables. But they don't *like* eating them, as to a cat, most fruits taste too sour, and most vegetables too bitter.

Pigs, on the other hand, *love* bitter flavours. To them, a half-rotten apple or potato might taste like ice cream . . .

Do pigs eat their own poo?

Pigs do sometimes eat their own poo. But they usually don't do it on purpose.

Some animals, like **rabbits**, eat their own poo so that they can digest it better. Rabbits eat tough, woody plants and grasses that are hard to break down in their little digestive systems. So they half digest the food on the first pass, poo out a little food pellet, eat it, then pass it through their guts a second time to finish the job. Rabbits probably don't *like* the taste of their own poo so much. But it doesn't seem to taste bad enough to stop them eating it.

Similarly, **pigs** probably don't really *like* the taste of their own poo. But they don't mind if there's a little poo on their food, either. They have strong digestive systems, so eating poo won't make them sick the way it would a human. And above all, pigs are survivors. They've evolved to eat whatever, whenever. Even if other animals turn their noses up at it.

Evolution, in fact, explains a lot about different animals' diets and tastes. For the most part, animals prefer foods that are commonly found in their surroundings. Or rather, the places where they evolved. After all, if they can't make use of the local food, most animals won't survive long enough to evolve into something else . . .

Planti-vores and Meati-vores

You've probably heard the words **carnivore** and **herbivore**.

Herbivores – like **cows**, **sheep**, **horses**, **antelopes** and **elephants** – eat **plants** and **plant parts** such as grasses, leaves, roots and shoots. This is one of the simplest ways to feed, provided there are plenty of plants about. (Being a herbivore is easy in grasslands and forests, but less so in deserts and the Arctic.) For this reason, cows, sheep, horses and other herbivores seem to prefer bitter-tasting plant foods to sour-tasting fruit or chunks of savoury tuna fish.

Carnivores – which include **cats**, **wolves**, **whales**, **weasels**, **sharks**, **snakes**, **eagles** and **crocodiles** – eat **other animals**. For this reason, they dislike the bitter taste of plants, but love the meaty, savoury taste of meat and fish.

There are other groups within these two main ones too. **Frugivores** are herbivores that eat **mostly fruits**. They prefer the sweet tastes of bananas, peaches and mangos. **Insectivores** are carnivores that – you guessed it – eat **mainly insects**. So they like the savoury, salty taste of ants, termites and big, juicy maggots.

The point is, each animal's sense of taste is shaped by the things it eats. **Sheep** have learned to *love* the taste of **grass** because that's all there was for them to eat. Likewise, **anteaters** have learned to *love* eating **ants**, and **shrews** have learned to *love* **worms** and **grubs**.

Who knows – with enough practice – maybe you'd learn to love eating maggots too . . .

BIG SENSE

Largest Tongue

Which animal has the largest tongue?

This prize goes to the largest animal on the planet, and quite possibly the largest animal that has ever lived – the blue whale. Adult blue whales reach a length of up to 108 feet (33m), and weigh up to 200 tons (180,000 kg). A **blue whale's tongue** alone **weighs over 2.7 tons**, and is about the same size and weight as an Indian elephant.

Which animal has the longest tongue?

TASTE

Many **moths** and **butterflies** have a spectacularly long tongue, or **proboscis**, which they dip deep into orchids and other plants to sip the nectar within. The **longest known insect tongue** belongs to the

Madagascan hawkmoth. Although large for a moth, its body is still only a few inches long, while its tongue measures almost **a foot (30 cm)** in length.

Among the reptiles, **chameleons** have famously long tongues. Some chameleons' tongues are longer than their bodies, at up to **53cm (21 inches)** long. They use their tongues like **sticky harpoons**, shooting them out to snag their prey – and sucking them back into their mouths – in the space of half a second. Small chameleons catch mostly flies, crickets and other insects. But larger species, like the panther chameleon, also wrap their sticky tongues around lizards, birds and rodents.

Giraffes and their relatives have some of the longest tongues among mammals. Giraffes use their long, **45cm (18-inch) tongues** to strip leaves from trees. Their relatives (they're from the same animal family – Giraffidae), **Okapi** – close relatives of giraffes – have long tongues too. Okapi live in the rainforests of Central Africa. Their bright blue tongues can reach up to 50cm (20 inches) in length – long enough to clean its own eyes and ears. *Now that'd be a neat trick to show your friends . . .*

But the **longest tongues** on land belong to **giant anteaters** and **pangolins**.

Giant anteaters live in Central and South America. As you might expect from their name, they flick their **61cm (24-inch) tongues** into ant and termite mounds to suck up tasty insects.

Giant pangolins are large, tree-climbing anteaters that live in West and Central Africa. At up to **70cm (28 inches)**, their tongues are even longer. Also, their bodies are covered with a layer of thick armour plating, made from hardened body hair. If you saw one, you might well mistake it for some sort of dinosaur!

What's the worst-tasting animal in the world?

Most of the world's poisonous or toxic plants, fungi and animals taste pretty bad. (After all, what's the point in being poisonous if you're also delicious?) The bright colourings of **sea snakes**, **poison arrow frogs** and **fly agaric mushrooms** all warn predators and grazers not to eat them. But many poisonous organisms *also* have a **bitter, unpleasant taste**. So even when some unfortunate animal scoops them into its mouth, they have one, final warning not to swallow.

But many **non-poisonous animals** use the 'Don't eat me – I taste terrible!' defence too. On land, **gastropods** (**slugs** and **snails**) produce a thick layer of **sticky, foul-tasting mucus** which covers their skins, and puts off all but the most determined bird.

Beneath the waves, **sea snakes, flatfish**, and **sea cucumbers** have evolved a range of awful flavours to deter sharks, dolphins and other ocean predators. The highly toxic **blue-ringed octopus** advertises its dangerousness with its bright blue-and-yellow spotted colouring, and with its revolting, bitter taste. Better pay attention too, as a single bite from its tiny beak can kill a healthy adult human in hours.

On the flipside, the clever **mimic octopus** isn't poisonous or dangerous at all. But, like other animals who are skilled at **camouflage**, when attacked it cleverly twists its tentacles into various shapes to impersonate sea snakes, lionfish, and other toxic animals. We don't know how bad the mimic octopus tastes if you eat one . . .

Which animal has the most sensitive tastes?

If you own a pet cat, you might think it's our fussy feline friends that have the most sensitive tongues. But in fact, **cats** only have about **400 taste buds** on their tongues, compared with **1,700** for a **dog**, and up to **9,000** for a **human**.

Believe it or not, **pigs** and **goats** each have over **15,000 taste buds** on their tongues, so probably have a better sense of taste than us. So do **rabbits**, with over **17,000 taste buds**, and **cows**, with over **25,000**! Just because they occasionally eat their own poo, that doesn't mean they can't appreciate a good meal.

The **best tasters** known on the planet are actually **catfish**, some of which have over **250,000 taste buds**! What's more, these taste buds are scattered *all over* the place – on the surface of their fins, tails, heads and bodies. They're basically

swimming tongues, and they use their acute sense to find and hoover up every last scrap of food in their river, lake or (if you have one at home) fish tank. Now I wonder what catfish taste like to cats . . .

Which animal has the least sensitive tastes?

The least fussy eaters on land are all **omnivores** – animals that eat leaves, roots, nuts, fruits, fish, meat and . . . well . . . pretty much anything, really.

Most **dogs** are omnivores. That includes pet dogs like labradors and terriers, but also wild dogs like wolves, dingoes and hyenas. Their fairly poorly developed taste buds make it easier for them to gobble down whatever is around. For wild hyenas, that might mean chomping down on the rotten carcass of a dead antelope. For pet dogs, that sometimes means crayons, cat litter and bits of string. (And none of these things are good for them – so be careful what you leave lying about!)

Goats, **pigs** and **bears** are also pretty unfussy eaters, and will eat more or less anything they can get their teeth into.

Out at sea, **Great White** and **bull sharks** aren't too fussy about what they swallow, either. Great Whites have been found with all sorts of things in their stomachs, including wallets, surfboards, fur coats, fishing rods, number plates, human skulls and up to three whole porpoises. This has earned them the nickname 'dustbins of the sea'. To a shark, apparently, everything tastes good . . .

TASTE

SPECIAL SENSE

Do butterflies like butter?

No, they don't. At least not especially.

Butterflies probably got their English name from the fact that many common European ones are a yellowish white, or **butter-coloured**. There's an old dairy farmer's legend that butterflies are really **witches** or **fairies** in disguise, who land on uncovered milk or butter and devour it! But in fact, most butterflies prefer **nectar** – the sugary liquid found within flowering plants.

Plants produce **nectar** to encourage **butterflies**, **moths**, **bees**, **bats**, **birds** and other animals to land on them. When this happens, the feeding animal is sneakily dabbed with **pollen** from the plant, which it then carries to the next plant it feeds on. Hopefully (for the plant), some of the pollen may then drop on to (or rub off on) this second plant and fertilize it, producing new seeds. This is called **pollination**.

Since plants can't move around for themselves, they use **pollinating insects** (and other animals) to carry their pollen around for them. In turn, the faithful pollen-porters get a tasty meal of *sweet nectar*. And the sweeter the nectar, the more likely it is than a butterfly will come calling.

Is that why butterflies have such long tongues?

Well, yes and no. Butterflies do have a very long, tube-like tongue called a **proboscis**. They keep it coiled up as they fly around, then unfurl it like a party streamer when they land on a flower – threading it deep into the flower and sipping nectar from it as if sipping a drink through a straw. But here's the thing: there are *no* taste buds on a butterfly's tongue. So how do they know which plants contain the tastiest nectar?

To begin with, they have a keen sense of **smell**, which guides them towards sweet-smelling flowers.

(The flowers, of course, have evolved their sweet smell for just that reason – to attract insects and advertise the tasty nectar fountain within.) Once they've followed the smell-trail to a flower, they land on its petals and get a taste of it straight away. How? They **taste it with their feet**.

Tasting with Toes

In reptiles, birds and mammals, the smell-sensors are in the nose, and the taste-sensors are in the mouth (mostly on the tongue). In **butterflies** and many **other insects**, however, the **smell-sensors sit on the *antennae***, and the **taste-sensors sit on their *legs* or *feet***.

These sensors are much like the taste cells and taste buds inside your mouth – they bind to certain chemicals, then pass messages on to the insect's brain if any tasty, 'foody' ones are recognized. Butterflies don't have the same range of tastes as we do, but are still very good at detecting the sweet-tasting plant sugars they crave, and the bitter-tasting plant poisons they would rather avoid.

If you think about it, this all makes sense. The butterfly hasn't got *time* to stop, land and dip its tongue into every flower it finds, to see if it's worth eating there. Instead, it lands, gets a quick taste of the flower's petals or leaves through its feet, then decides if it's worth unrolling its tongue and going for a dip.

Butterflies also use their toe-tasters to weigh up how tasty and nutritious a plant's leaves might be for its young. Before a female butterfly lays its eggs, it lands on many different plants, tasting its leaves with its feet. From a quick landing, it can tell if the plant would be a healthy food source for its baby caterpillars, or whether the plant is rotten, infected or diseased. If it finds a good, healthy one with the right 'flavour', it lays its eggs there, and the caterpillars that hatch from them find an enormous, delicious leafy buffet waiting for them.

All in all, it's not a bad being a butterfly, really.
You're born, you wriggle around gorging yourself
on tasty leaves, and when you can't eat any more,
you wrap yourself in a snug cocoon and go to sleep.
Then when you wake up, you can fly, you can taste
things with your feet, and you spend all day looking
at pretty flowers and sipping sugar-water. Life could
be a lot worse . . .

COMMON SENSE

CHAPTER 5: TOUCH

COMMON SENSE

Do all animals touch and feel things?

Yes, they do. It's not just animals that do it, either. **Plants** use a sense of touch to avoid growing too close to each other, and to wrap their vines around tree trunks and trellises. **Fungi** use a touch sense to cluster together into one big, mouldy mass. Even **bacteria** use touch-sensors to sense the surfaces they grow on. In fact, pretty much every living thing on the planet uses some sort of touchy-feely sense to live and survive.

Touch evolved long before vision or hearing in animals. The first animal eyes didn't appear until about 500 million years ago. Before that, the only way an animal could know where it was – or where it was going – was to *feel* its way about. Even today, touch is still an important way for animals to sense the world around them.

Could you live without being able to touch things?

It's possible, but not likely. If you think about it, from the moment you wake up in the morning to the moment you fall asleep, your body is touching and sensing something around you. Unless, perhaps, you're an astronaut floating about in space. But even then, your sense of touch tells you you've still got your spacesuit on!

Down here on Earth, **gravity** is constantly pulling us towards the ground. When we're lying down, this presses our whole bodies into the ground, and the ground presses back against our bodies. When we sit up, the ground presses against the skin of our bottoms. When we crawl, the ground presses against our hands and knees. And when we stand, walk, run or jump, it presses (harder at some times, lighter at others) against the soles of our feet.

Without being able to feel this pressure on our

TOUCH

135

bottoms, hands, knees and feet, it would be almost impossible to sit, stand, crawl, walk, run or jump properly.

Have you ever felt your legs 'go to sleep'?

When you sit cross-legged or with your legs raised for a long period of time, the bloodflow to your legs decreases, and the nerves don't work as well. This can make your legs (for a little while, at least) feel numb, or as if they're made of wood. When you try to get up, you wobble all over the place, as your brain isn't getting the signals it needs from your feet to help keep you balanced. So you can hardly stay standing, let alone walk, run or jump!

Just think how difficult life would be if your legs were like that *all the time*. Well, without working touch-sensors and nerves, they would be. For this and other reasons, the skin of our bottoms, knees, feet and hands are *covered* with **touch-sensors**, and *riddled* with **sensitive nerves**.

How do we touch and feel things?

Your sense of **touch** is related to your sense of **hearing**. Both sense changes in vibration or pressure, and turn that sensation into a message sent to the brain. Your **skin** senses **contact** and **pressure** as it is stretched or pressed. Similarly, your **ears** sense **sounds**, which are changes in the air or water pressure around you, as they bend and stretch your eardrums and wobble the bones and hairs behind. So in a way, hearing is like 'touching at a distance'. In fact hearing evolved from the sense of touch, which came earlier. And both use the same sorts of touchy-feely sensors to do it.

Touch-sensors

Here's how touch works. Whenever you touch something – like pressing your fingertip on to a table, or pressing your foot into the ground – it stretches the skin around the point of contact. As the skin s t r e t c h e s, tiny touch-sensors (called **mechanoreceptors**) inside the skin get stretched and squashed too.

Each one of these little touch-sensitive patches has a **nerve** attached to it, and when the sensor is stretched or squashed, it fires off a **signal** through that nerve to the brain. The brain recognizes this as 'pressure' or 'contact'. The harder the skin is pressed, the more the sensors inside it stretch, and the more signals they send to the brain. A light touch sends a lazy stream of light 'pings' to the brain, while a heavy press (or a hard knock) fires a barrage of signals like a machine gun.

The same thing happens whether *you* touch something or whether *something* touches you. If someone presses the tip of a pencil into your hand, for example, it creates a little, stretchy dent or crater in the skin. As the skin in and around the dent stretches, the touch-sensors inside fire off signals, just like before (try this for yourself, but don't press too hard).

Rough, smooth, sticky and slippery

There are different types of touch-sensors within your skin. Some just sense **contact** and **pressure**, while others sense **textures** – how rough, smooth, sticky or slippery a surface is. These work a little differently.

When you run your finger over a piece of rough wood, these sensors detect the vibration in the skin of your fingertip as it travels over tiny lumps and bumps in the surface of the wood. If the surface has lots of lumps and bumps then the skin vibrates a lot, and the sensors send signals to the brain that say '**rough**'. If there are very few bumps – such as on the surface of a polished, metal mirror – there's very little vibration, and the sensors send signals that say '**smooth**'.

The same sensors also detect how easily the skin slips and slides over a surface. If the skin glides easily across it, they signal the brain, saying '**slippery**' or '**wet**'. If the skin gets caught and judders across the surface in little jumps, they send signals saying '**sticky**'.

Living with touch alone

Some animals depend far more on their sense of touch than others. Not all animals have eyes, or live in environments in which eyes are that useful. As you might expect, animals that live and hunt during the daytime (**diurnal animals**) don't use their touch-sensors as much as animals that live and hunt by night (**nocturnal animals**). And many animals that live in pitch-black caves, or deep underground, use their sense of touch instead of their eyes, since their eyes are useless without light anyway.

Animals with a very sensitive sense of touch have many **more touch-sensors** in their skin (or certain bits of their skin) than we humans do. Even for us, our touch-sensors aren't spread out evenly. The skin on our **elbows**, **backs** and **bellies** contains **hundreds of touch-sensors** per square centimetre. But the skin on our **fingers, hands**, **toes**, **fingers**, **faces**, **eyelids** and **lips** have **thousands** per square centimetre.

This makes sense for us, as we tend to explore the world with our sensitive hands and feet. Having sensitive eyelids and cheeks, meanwhile, reminds us to protect our eyes and brains from injury, and sensitive lips help prevent us from eating anything too rough or sharp to pass safely through our throats, stomachs and guts.

All in all, it's a big touchy feely world.

ANIMAL SENSE

How do moles see underground?

For the most part, they don't.

This is not because they lack the equipment. Most moles do tend to have extremely small eyes, sometimes even covered with skin. But they're *not completely blind*. All moles can tell night from day at the surface, and in full daylight, some can even spot insects and worms over short distances. That said, when they're tunnelling underground, where no light can penetrate, their eyes are useless. Which is why, of course, they use a different tactic . . .

TOUCH

Moles are the **touchy-feely masters** of the mammal world. Their hairless noses are covered with hundreds (or even thousands) of tiny, fleshy buttons called **Eimer's organs**. Each little button is covered with **touch-sensors** and **nerve endings**. With just a quick brush of these nose-mounted super-sensors against an object, a mole can tell immediately what it has found (such as a leaf, a worm or an insect larva) and where it is within its tunnels.

Tunnel Vision

European moles dig huge tunnel systems underground, with wide chambers connected by thin tunnels that can cover **hundreds of square metres**. They need this wide area so that they can find enough prey (**earthworms**, **beetles**, **spiders** and other munchables) to feed themselves each day, and they spend most of each day patrolling and maintaining their tunnels. At intervals, worms and insects wriggle from the soil and drop into their tunnels, and moles have to be quick to scoop them up before they dig their way out again.

But *how* do the moles know which way they're going on their tunnel patrols? After all, with no underground map they could end up running around the same bit of tunnel all day, and miss all the tasty food dropping into the other bits.

Well, for starters, the walls of every tunnel and chamber have their own, unique sandy or gritty feel. To us, they would look and feel the same. But to a mole's **super-sensitive nose**, they're like road signs or trail markers. A quick brush against the wall, and the mole knows which tunnel it's running through and which direction it's taking through it.

What's more, they don't just run through the tunnels all day, hoping to find their prey. The mole's nose is so sensitive that it can '**remote-touch**', or 'feel at a distance'. By touching its nose to the tunnel wall or floor, a mole can feel the **vibrations** caused by a **wriggling worm** or **scampering beetle** several metres away – whether it has already dropped into the mole's tunnels, or is in the soil round about them.

The world champion nose-feelers are **star-nosed moles**, which live in Eastern Canada and the USA. This mole gets its name from the **star-shaped ring of tentacles** on its snout.

Between them, these 22 tentacles hold over **25,000 Eimer's organs**, which twitch and wriggle in constant motion. These allow the star-nosed mole to 'see' underground almost as well as we see above ground with our eyes. With instant updates from their questing nose-tentacles, they can 'map' their tunnels in seconds, detect prey at amazing distances, and even detect prey underwater. Star-nosed moles – like their cousins, the **desmans** – are expert swimmers, and they use their tentacled feelers to hunt water snails, leeches and small fish in freshwater streams.

More Touchy Animals

Moles aren't the only animals to use their noses like eyes, either. The odd, **duck-like bill** of the **playtpus** is actually a huge, touch-sensitive plate. The **50,000 touch-sensors** on its surface work a little differently, but the idea is the same. The platypuses use these much like the star-nosed mole's tentacles to sense tiny changes in water pressure that give away the presence of scuttling shrimp, crayfish and insect larvae underwater. Amazingly, platypuses can also detect the tiny electric currents given off by their prey's twitching muscles. As it hunts, the platypus skims the river bed with its bill, digging up silt and sweeping its bill from side to side like a radar dish until it detects its prey. Which just goes to show – almost anything can look funny until you understand what it's there for!

Many shorebirds, such as **sandpipers** and **oystercatchers**, also use touch-sensors on their **long**, **probing beaks** to feel around for prey beneath the sand. Like moles and platypuses, their touch-sensitive noses can feel movement and pressure at a distance. So a quick prod and shuffle through the sand can reveal the solid shape of an oyster, or the movement of a wriggling worm, more than a foot (30cm) away. Flightless **kiwis** use a similar tactic to find grubs and insects in loose soil and leaf litter in the forests of New Zealand. These birds rely upon their **touch-sensitive beaks** to live and survive – if you think about it, they probably wouldn't have too much luck just jabbing away with their beaks at random . . .

Why do cats have whiskers?

Whiskers are basically **face-mounted feelers** for sensing objects, air currents and water currents around an animal's head. It's not just cats that have them, either. While birds, reptiles and amphibians do not have them, whiskers and hair are found throughout the entire mammal family. **Dogs**, **wolves**, **bears**, **seals** and many other **carnivores** have them. As do **mice**, **hamsters**, **gerbils**, **rabbits** and other **herbivores**.

Zoologists *used* to think that animals used them to sense how wide gaps were (and whether the animal could fit its body through), or to avoid bumping their heads into things in the dark. But we *now* know that whiskers (along with **sensory hairs** elsewhere on the body) do *much* more than that.

How whiskers work

The base of each single hair (known as a **hair follicle**) sits beneath the surface of the skin. It is surrounded by a tiny, fluid-filled bag, with a number of touch-sensors on each side. When the end of the hair (outside the skin) is bent over, the base of the hair (beneath the skin) shifts in the opposite direction, like a see-saw.

As it does so, it presses into the fluid around it, which in turn presses into the touch-sensors all around. The sensors then send signals to the brain, telling it where the pressure is coming from. This turns hair, fur and whiskers into **touch-sensing antennae**, and many animals use them to sense wind currents, water currents and the movement of animals they are hunting.

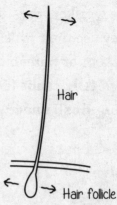

Hair

Hair follicle

Whiskers – or **fibrissae**, as biologists call them – are the largest and most sensitive sensory hairs. On land, they're used by **nocturnal scamperers** like **shrews** and **mice** to sense predators stalking them in the darkness. When a nervous mouse twitches its whiskers, it's sensing tiny shifts in air pressure around it that might give away the presence of a large body (say, a hungry cat) nearby. In turn, **nocturnal predators** – like **cats**, **civets**, **raccoons** and **weasels** – use their whiskers to sense the tiny shifts in air pressure caused by the scurrying movements of their prey.

Underwater carnivores, like **seals** and **otters**, use whiskers too. Instead of sensing air currents, they use their whiskers to sense changes in water pressure or water currents, which allows them to hunt **fish**, **crabs** (and in the case of the leopard seal, **penguins**!) underwater in near darkness.

BIG SENSE

Which animal has the longest whiskers?

Shrews – relatives of mice, rats and other rodents – have the longest whiskers relative to their body size. The pygmy shrew's body is just 3–5cm (1.5–2 inches) long, yet its whiskers span almost the same distance. This would be like a cat with whiskers of about 50 cm (20 inches) across.

The longest whiskers on the planet belong to **Antarctic fur seals**, whose longest whiskers reach up to **50cm (20 inches)**, giving them a total whisker-span of 1 metre (3 feet)!

Longest Whiskers

Which animal has the most arms?

The touchy-feely **octopus** has, famously, **eight 'arms'** or tentacles. Each one is covered with two to three rows of **sticky suckers**, which the octopus can contract at will in order to **touch**, **grab** and **manipulate** things. But octopuses are not the only animals with multiple arms or tentacles –

TOUCH

nor do they have the most per animal.

Squid have eight tentacles covered with hooks or suckers, plus an additional two arms (usually, a bit longer than the rest), giving **a total 'arm count' of 10**. They also use their arms a little differently. Octopuses use all eight tentacles to capture their prey, then bite or inject venom to finish it off. Squid, however, tend to use their two longest arms to reach out and capture prey, then hold it still with the other arms while they rip their prey apart. Nasty.

Most **starfish** – and their cousins, the **brittle stars** – have five 'arms', but some have **50 'arms'** or more. Each arm has hundreds of tiny, tentacled feelers on the lower side. Since they use these feelers mainly for walking, most biologists think of them as 'feet'. But starfish also use them to grab their prey (anemones or shellfish), rip them off rocks, lever their shells open, and stuff bits into their mouths.

Speaking of **anemones**, if tentacles count as 'arms', then they take the prize for **'best armed animal'**. Some sea anemones have up to **1,000 grasping, waving tentacles**, making them the hands-down winners!

Which animal has the longest arms?

All **apes** (including us) have pretty long arms –
a hangover from our tree-swinging ancestors.
Humans have an average armspan (the distance
from fingertip to fingertip with both arms
outstretched) of **1.7m (5.5 feet)**.

Bandy-armed **siamang gibbons** are less than
half our height, yet with an armspan of **1.5m
(5 feet)**, their arms are almost as long as ours!

The longest arms on *land* belong to fully grown
mountain gorillas and **orangutans**, which have
incredible armspans of up to **3m (or 9 feet)**.

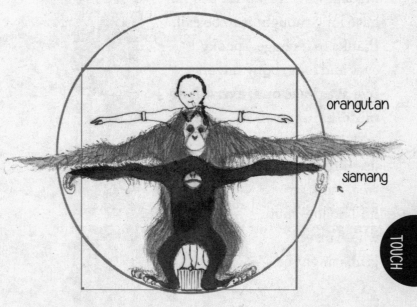

orangutan

siamang

If **tentacles** count as arms, then the longest on the *planet* clearly belong to the **giant squid**, whose tentacles measure up to **8m (27 feet)** long.

Which animal has the longest fingers?

The **aye-aye** a small, strange-looking lemur that lives only in the mountain forests of Madagascar. The native people have long thought it to be evil, thanks to its huge, spooky eyes and long, bony fingers. Aye-ayes have **one, *extra-long* middle finger** on each hand. They use it to tap on tree trunks to find hollow spots where insect grubs might be hiding, to poke around inside trees and fish them out.

Green iguanas have long, clawed fingers for grasping and climbing trees. Adult iguanas grow up to 2.1m (7 feet) in length, and their fingers are longer than those of an adult human.

The longest fingers, though, belong to **bats**, whose fingers have stretched out to support the thin, leathery membranes of their wings. The largest of the fruit bat family – the **greater flying fox** – has a wingspan of over **1.8m (6 feet)**, and the longest fingers supporting each wing measure over **45cm (1.5 feet)** from base to fingertip.

SPECIAL SENSE

Why do spiders make webs?

Spiders are masters of '**long-distance touch**', and when they build webs, it's partly to extend the reach of their powerful touch sense far beyond their bodies.

Not all spiders build webs. Some, like **jumping spiders** and **tarantulas**, simply stalk and pounce on their prey like miniature, eight-legged leopards. Others, like **trapdoor spiders**, hide in underground burrows and wait until an unfortunate beetle scuttles past before pouncing. Like predatory reptiles, birds and mammals, these hunting spiders tend to have fairly good eyesight for stalking their prey.

Web-building spiders are different. Like moles, they tend to have poor vision. They can tell night from day, and make things out a few centimetres in front of them. But beyond that, it's all a blur. Instead, like moles, they rely on remote touch to find their prey. And they do it in a very special way.

Deadly nets

Web facts:

- Spiders spin their webs using fine (but amazingly strong) silk threads squeezed from special organs in their abdomens.
- Some build a new web every day, eating yesterday's web every night and spinning a new one every morning.
- Others build webs that last for weeks or months.
- Webs vary in size from a few centimetres to almost 3 metres (10 feet) across. Recently, biologists discovered a species of orb-weaving spider in Madagascar (called **Darwin's bark spider**) that weaves a web over 2.8m (9 feet) wide, which it hangs over wide rivers and streams to catch flying insects.

TOUCH

Spider webs are *more* than just big, sticky nets for catching prey. When combined with the spider's amazing sense of touch, they become an extension of the spider's brain – like thin, silky hands with fingers outstretched.

Spiders, as we all know, have eight pairs of legs – each one tipped with hairs and hooks that help it stick to walls, and that help it sense its environment. But these are just the walking legs. In front of these, there are two more pairs of limbs. One pair (called **chelicerae**) sit either side of the mouth, and are used for breaking up food and stuffing it into the mouth. People often mistake these for teeth – as they look like huge fangs when you see them up close. But they're actually stubby, limbs modified for grabbing.

Between these 'grabbers' and the walking legs are another pair of limbs called **pedipalps**. These are covered in touch-sensors and loaded with nerve endings, making them as sensitive as the mole's nose or kiwi's beak.

Feely-trap

After a web-building spider spins its web, it sits in the middle (or off to one side) with its touchy-feely pedipalps resting on a web line. Through this, the spider can 'see' its entire web by feel alone. Even the tiniest vibration of a feather-winged moth or a tiny gnat feels like an earth tremor to the waiting spider.

Even in total darkness, the spider's brain sees its web completely clearly – as you would see your hands before your face in bright daylight. Once trapped, the prey has no chance of escape. The spider scuttles to the source of the struggle, injects it venom, and paralyses its prey. This done, it may eat it right away, or just wrap it in silk and save it for later – moving back to its favourite spot to wait for more helpless victims to fall into its silken fingers.

Every species of web-building spider has its own, unique web pattern. Many spiders build webs shaped like **small, circular nets**. But others have webs shaped like **sheets**, **cones**, **tubes**, **funnels**, **tents** and **domes**. Many spider families – such as **funnel-web spiders** – are named after the types of web they build. Some **cobweb spiders** work together and build their webs side-by-side, creating enormous '**superwebs**' **100m (300 feet)** or more across.

Most amazingly of all, some **water spiders** use the still surfaces of freshwater ponds as their webs. They rest their super-sensitive pedipalp legs on the surface of the water to feel for tiny ripples in the pond. When a small, flying insect accidentally plops into the water, it becomes trapped in its surface tension and creates ripples as it struggles to free itself. But its struggles don't last long. Once it feels the vibrations, the water spider will scuttle across the surface of the water like an Olympic ice skater, plucking the insect from the pond and delivering a deadly bite.

With their **super-sensitive touch**, spiders are among the most successful hunters on the planet. There are over 35,000 species of spider in the world, and billions of individual spiders out there hunting. Between them, they catch an incredible number of insects. So many, in fact, that if you placed the total number of insects the world's spiders capture and eat each year on a scale, it would be heavier than the total weight of human beings on the planet.

Without them, the world would be a much creepier, crawlier place.

So next time you're thinking of washing a spider down the plughole, have a think about that.

GRARRR!

SUPER GEEK!

DINOSAURS, BRAINS AND SUPERTRAINS

THE WORLD CANNOT SURVIVE WITHOUT THE WISDOM OF
THE QUICK-WITTED GEEK. HOW MUCH DO *YOU*
REALLY KNOW ABOUT THE SCIENCE THAT MATTERS?

WHAT KIND OF ANIMAL WAS A *MEGALODON*?
HOW LONG COULD YOU SURVIVE WITH ONLY *HALF* A BRAIN?
HOW LARGE WOULD AN ASTEROID HAVE TO BE TO
WIPE OUT ALL HUMAN LIFE ON THE PLANET?

FIND OUT THE ANSWERS TO THESE AND AN AWFUL LOT OF
OTHER BRILLIANT QUESTIONS IN THIS BRAIN-BOGGLING QUIZ
BOOK WHICH WILL TEST THE BRAINIEST OF SUPERGEEKS.
ARE YOU GEEK ENOUGH?

GLENN MURPHY, AUTHOR OF **WHY IS SNOT GREEN?**, SETS THE
QUESTIONS AND GIVES THE ANSWERS IN THIS FUN-FILLED
BOOK OF CHALLENGES WITH NO BORING BITS!

GLENN MURPHY

SUPER GEEK!

ROBOTS, SPACE and FURRY ANIMALS

THE WORLD CANNOT SURVIVE WITHOUT THE WISDOM OF
THE QUICK-WITTED GEEK. HOW MUCH DO YOU
REALLY KNOW ABOUT THE SCIENCE THAT MATTERS?

HOW LONG WOULD IT TAKE A MANNED SPACECRAFT TO REACH MARS?
COULD YOU SHOW US WHERE YOUR SPLEEN IS?
HOW MANY ROBOTS ARE LIVING IN THE WORLD TODAY?
WHERE DOES A *PANGOLIN* LIVE?

FIND OUT THE ANSWERS TO THESE AND AN AWFUL LOT OF
OTHER BRILLIANT QUESTIONS IN THIS BRAIN-BOGGLING QUIZ
BOOK WHICH WILL TEST THE BRAINIEST OF SUPERGEEKS.
ARE YOU GEEK ENOUGH?

GLENN MURPHY, AUTHOR OF WHY IS SNOT GREEN?, SETS THE
QUESTIONS AND GIVES THE ANSWERS IN THIS FUN-FILLED
BOOK OF CHALLENGES WITH NO BORING BITS!

GLENN MURPHY

SPACE

THE WHOLE WHIZZ-BANG STORY

WHAT IS THE UNIVERSE?
WHAT WOULD HAPPEN IF YOU WERE FLYING
A SPACESHIP NEAR A BLACK HOLE?
HOW DO WE KNOW THAT STARS AND GALAXIES
ARE BILLIONS OF YEARS OLD?

GLENN MURPHY ANSWERS THESE AND A LOT OF OTHER BRILLIANT
QUESTIONS IN THIS FUNNY AND INFORMATIVE BOOK.

PACKED WITH INFORMATION, PUZZLES, QUIZZES, PHOTOS
AND DOODLES ABOUT ALL SORTS OF INCREDIBLE THINGS
LIKE SUPERMASSIVE BLACK HOLES, GALAXIES, TELESCOPES,
PLANETS, SOLAR FLARES, CONSTELLATIONS, ECLIPSES AND RED
DWARFS, THIS BOOK HAS NO BORING BITS!

By me,
GLENN MURPHY